Irish Planning and Acquisition Law

Philip O'Sullivan

Institute of Public Administration
Dublin

Published by
Institute of Public Administration
57-61 Lansdowne Road
Dublin 4
Ireland

ISBN 0 902173 80 4

First published 1978

Printed in Ireland by
Mount Salus Press, Sandymount, Dublin

Preface

This book is written primarily with the student in mind and deals with developments in Irish planning and compulsory purchase law in the last decade or so. It would not have been attempted without the encouragement of Brendan Kiernan, sometime legal adviser to the then Department of Local Government and now a member of the European Commission of Human Rights, or my colleague Ernán P. de Blaghd, Barrister-at-law, both of whom read the text and made many helpful suggestions. I would also like to thank my painstaking publisher, and Frances Horgan for typing the text.

Contents

CHAPTER ONE

Judicial Control of the Administration

The nineteenth century was the age of the individual *par excellence.* It is therefore not surprising that one aspect of law which developed especially rapidly in that century was contract law, the law governing the freely adopted legal relations between individuals. In English law private property was still regarded as almost sacrosanct and the *laissez-faire* economic theory of the time was inspired by the view that the individual's self-interest, if left alone, would provide such stimulus as the economy required. Even Darwin's theory of the evolution of the species placed an emphasis on the struggle of the individual for survival.

No doubt this is a selective characterisation of the nineteenth century but it serves to contrast it with the present age which has seen the emergence and development of the welfare state. The paternalism of the modern state dictates that the weak, the incapacitated, the aged and the disabled will be supported in need by state funds and state services, which in the long term means by money and resources provided by the fit and able members of society. One has only to think of the curtailment of property rights effected by our planning law or the merger in practice of the individual's rights as a worker in trade unions,[1] and the fact that the long tax-collecting arm of the state is elbow deep in our pockets to pay for its benevolent enterprises, to see at once this difference between the two centuries.[2]

However, the *laissez-faire* economy contained within itself the seed of its own destruction. In the wake of the industrial revolution in England came the rapid and confused expansion of urban centres bringing with it what would now be regarded as community problems. Inevitably, local and central authorities discovered that they had to intervene if primeval chaos was to be avoided. For example, regulations had to be made about such things as habitable and sanitary housing and children's working hours.

One specific example[3] of this kind of law occurred in an English Act of 1855 which provided that anyone wishing to erect a building in London had first to give seven days notice to the local Board of Works, failing which, the Board could demolish the building. Within eight years of the passing of this Act, one Cooper started to build a house without giving the statutory notice. When his building had reached the second storey, the Board moved in late one night and proceeded to demolish it. Cooper took the case to court where it was decided by an unanimous Court of Common Pleas that, despite the fact that the Board of Works was doing exactly what Parliament had said it could do, nonetheless, it had exercised its authority in the wrong way: it had failed to give Cooper notice of its intentions and an opportunity to put his side of the case thereby offending against one of the two primary rules of natural justice, *audi alteram partem.*[4]

This case provides an example of the making by Parliament of a regulatory statute, the apparent breach of it by a citizen, and an adjudication of the subsequent contest between the parties by the courts—all within a decade. The judges had no difficulty in applying to this field of law the principles of procedural justice established outside it and it is true to say that in England and even more so in Ireland[5] 'administrative law' is neither a body of special rules nor the application of general rules in special courts but rather the application of ordinary legal principles to the administration which is subject to the control of the ordinary judges.

While, therefore, the emergence of administrative law is something which can be understood as an inevitable by-product of the welfare state, no intellectually satisfying definition of the subject can be offered which would mark off the boundaries of this field of law, as can be done, for example, in the cases of contract or company law.

Administrative law is concerned chiefly with the interaction between the individual and the agencies of the community, such as local and central authorities, and the topics dealt with in this book are affected by the procedural principles governing this interaction which have been set out or adopted by Irish judges.

A central question which arises is the extent to which the courts will control the administration in its exercise of the increasing power which it is assuming. Do the rules of natural justice apply to administrative authorities and, if so, to which of their functions? Does a power conferred by statute on an administrative authority have limits other than those defined in the authorising statute?

Not only is Irish administrative law ill-suited to conceptual definition, but even the contents of the subject may not be confidently asserted because this branch of law is undergoing rapid development and any book on the subject must necessarily be selective. Irish judges have been increasingly ready to assert their authority over both the Oireachtas and the administration and in this they have been doing no more than they are required to do by the Constitution.[6] One commentator[7] has compared the Irish courts in this regard with those in the United States, where it will be remembered that the Warren Supreme Court in the mid 1960s played a distinctively active part in determining how the country was run.

The relationship between the judiciary and parliament here can be contrasted with the position in Britain where constitutional authors refer correctly to the 'supremacy of Parliament'. There is no written British Constitution and any contest between Parliament and judiciary in that country must inevitably be won by Parliament.[8] Not so in Ireland. Several Acts of the Oireachtas have been declared unconstitutional in the Irish courts[9] and no attempt by the Oireachtas to avoid the principle underlying such a declaration can withstand challenge in the courts.

Further, the fact that the Constitution provides for a separation of powers,[10] as well as the exclusive exercise by the courts of an unlimited judicial power,[11] has enabled judges to adopt the authoritative line[12] with the administration required by the Constitution.[13] Indeed one writer[14] in discussing the case *Byrne v. Ireland* has suggested that in certain circumstances it is the duty of the court to invent appropriate relief when the same is not already provided. This duty, it is suggested, is imposed by article 40.3 which requires the state to vindicate a citizen's right in the case of injustice:

> But it is also arguable that, as, traditionally, no claim lay against the state for the torts of its servants, what the court was doing was inventing a new remedy. In other words, it is arguable that, because the court felt that Miss Byrne had a moral right to compensation from the state, it in-

vented a remedy to give her relief. Indeed, if a Constitution guarantees the natural right of each citizen to his property and if, as appears to be the case, article 40, section 3, obliges the state to vindicate his right in the case of injustice done, then it would appear that the court had no choice but to invent appropriate relief. *Ubi jus ibi remedium.*

One celebrated example of the readiness of Irish judges to take an assertive line in upholding the Constitution occurred in the case of *Ryan* v. *Attorney General*[15] where Kenny J., following an *obiter dictum* of Kingsmill-Moore J.,[16] ruled that the category of personal rights specified in article 40 of the Constitution is not exhaustive:

> In my opinion, the High Court has jurisdiction to consider whether an act of the Oireachtas respects, and as far as practicable, defends and vindicates the personal rights of the citizen and to declare the legislation unconstitutional if it does not. I think that the personal rights which may be invoked to invalidate legislation are not confined to those specified in article 40 but include all those rights which result from the Christian and democratic nature of the state . . . The High Court and the Supreme Court have the difficult and responsible duty of ascertaining and declaring what are the personal rights of the citizen which are guaranteed by the Constitution.[17]

In this case Kenny J. identified a right to bodily integrity as one of the personal rights of the citizen protected by the Constitution. He suggested further that the right to free movement within the state and the right to marry are also protected by article 40.

Another example of an assertive interpretation of the scope of constitutional protection occurs in the judgment of the same judge in the case *Central Dublin Development Association Ltd.* v. *Attorney General:*[18]

> In my view, an analysis of the text of the Constitution and of the decisions on it leads to these conclusions:
> (1) The right of private property is a personal right
> (2) In virtue of his rational being, man has a natural right to individual or private ownership of worldly wealth
> (3) This constitutional right consists of a bundle of rights most of which are found in contract
> (4) The state cannot pass any law which abolishes all the bundle of rights
> (5) The exercise of these rights ought to be regulated by the principles of social justice, and the state, accordingly, may by law restrict their exercise with a view to reconciling this with the demands of the common good
> (6) The courts have jurisdiction to enquire whether the restriction is in accordance with the principles of social justice and whether the legislation is necessary to reconcile this exercise with the demands of the common good

(7) If any of the rights which together constitute our conception of ownership are abolished or restricted (as distinct from the abolition of all the rights) the absence of compensation for this restriction or abolition will make the Act which does this, invalid, if it is an unjust attack on property rights.

In the case of *McGee* v. *Attorney General*,[19] a right to privacy or at least to marital privacy was vindicated and protected by the Supreme Court as appears, for example, from the following passage from the judgment of Walsh J.:

It is outside the authority of the state to endeavour to intrude into the privacy of the husband and wife relationship for the sake of imposing a code of private morality upon that husband and wife which they do not desire.

In my view, article 41 of the Constitution guarantees the husband and wife against any such invasion of their privacy by the state. It follows that the use of contraceptives by them within that marital privacy is equally guaranteed against such invasion and, as such, assumes the status of a right so guaranteed by the Constitution. If this right cannot be directly invaded by the state it follows that it cannot be frustrated by the state taking measures to ensure that the exercise of that right is rendered impossible.[20]

Indeed the judgment of Walsh J. in this case is remarkable also for the following passage, which gives clear expression to the view, firmly established since the judgments in *Byrne* v. *Ireland*,[21] that the state's powers of government can only be exercised through the appropriate organ established under the Constitution and that the individual has natural and human rights guaranteed and recognised by the Constitution over which the state has no authority:

Articles 40, 41, 42 and 44 of the Constitution all fall within that Section of the Constitution which is titled "Fundamental Rights". Articles 41, 42 and 43 emphatically reject the theory that there are no rights without laws, no rights contrary to the law and no rights anterior to the law. They indicate that justice is placed above the law and acknowledge that natural rights, or human rights, are not created by law but the constitution confirms their existence and gives them protection. The individual has natural and human rights over which the state has no authority; and the family, as the natural, primary and fundamental unit group of society, has rights as such which the state cannot control. However, at the same time it is true, as the Constitution acknowledges and claims, that the state is the guardian of the common good and that the individual, as a member of society, and the family, as a unit of society, have duties and obligations to consider and respect the common good of that society. It is important to recall that under the Constitution the state's powers of government are exercised in their respective spheres by the legislative, executive and judicial organs established under the Constitution. I agree with the view expressed by O'Byrne J. in *Buckley & Others (Sinn Féin)* v. *Attorney General*[22] that the power of the state to act for the protection of the common good or to decide what are the exigencies of the common good is not one which is peculiarly reserved for the legislative organ of government, in that the decision of the legislative organ is not absolute and is subject to and capable of being reviewed by the courts. In concrete terms that means that the legislature is not free to encroach unjustifiably upon the fundamental rights of individuals or of the family in the name of the common good, or by act or omission to abandon or to neglect the common good or the protection or enforcement of the rights of individual citizens.[23]

There is every inducement and jurisdiction, therefore, for Irish judges to adopt a questioning posture towards the institutions of our society and it is not surprising to find them adopting a critical and authoritative attitude towards the acts and powers of the administration.

Even at common law, without benefit of a written constitution guaranteeing the individual's fundamental rights, judges exercised certain controls over the administration such as the application of the rules of natural justice to judicial acts[24] or the review of the formal jurisdiction of administrative authorities when challenged under the prerogative procedures.[25]

Irish judges have in recent times extended the traditional grounds upon which such review will be exercised and have in certain cases tested the validity of acts or decisions by reference to criteria other than formalities.[26]

The fundamental relationship between the Irish courts and the other organs of the state and indeed that between the courts and the state itself was the subject of wide-ranging discussion in the judgments delivered in the case of *Byrne* v. *Ireland*.[27] In that case it was held that the former prerogative of immunity from suit in tort actions no longer protected the state of Ireland, that the state is a legal person which is vicariously liable for the tortious acts of its servants and that the courts have jurisdiction to deal with a claim for damages for such a tort. It was further held that the Attorney General is the appropriate person to represent the state in defending such a claim and that any order for damages will be made against the state itself.[28]

This assertive approach of the Irish courts towards the administration has produced significant decisions in the fields of compulsory acquisition of land by local authorities and of planning and development. This book deals with these decisions and includes an account of the planning code generally as extended by the Local Government (Planning and Development) Act 1976.

CHAPTER TWO

Compulsory Acquisition:
Procedural Principles

The procedures for compulsory acquisition of land by local authorities in this country have been largely standardised by section 86 of the Housing Act 1966, which entitles acquiring authorities to operate the Housing Act procedures set out in the Third Schedule to that Act when this is considered convenient.

This Schedule deals with the form which a compulsory purchase order shall take, the serving of notices on parties entitled to notice, the advertisement of the proposed confirmation by the Minister of the order made by the local authority (under the Housing and Planning Acts, the relevant Minister is the Minister for Local Government — since July 1977 styled Minister for the Environment), the making of objections by parties entitled to object and the holding and conduct of public local inquiries into such objections.

Major developments in the law of this country have occurred within the past five years or so by way of judicial interpretation of these and associated procedures but especially by way of judicial interpretation of article 5(2) of this Schedule. The sub-article reads as follows:

> (2) The Minister shall not confirm a compulsory purchase order in so far as it relates to any land in respect of which an objection is duly made by any of the persons upon whom notices of the making of the order are required to be served until he has caused to be held a public local inquiry into such objection and until he has considered such objection and the report of the person who held the inquiry, unless:
> (a) such objection is withdrawn, or
> (b) the Minister is satisfied that the objection relates exclusively to matters which can be dealt with by the arbitrator by whom the compensation may have to be assessed.

It will be seen from the above quotation that the onus is on the Minister not to confirm a compulsory purchase order until he has considered an objection and the report of the inspector who held a public local inquiry into it. The decision whether or not to confirm a compulsory purchase order is the Minister's and his alone but once an objection has been lodged he is obliged to consider it together with the report referred to.

As repeated reference will be made in this chapter to several cases taken by a builder named Joseph Murphy against Dublin Corporation and the Minister for Local Government,[1] the context in which these cases arose is now set out.

Mr Murphy was the owner of lands in north county Dublin over which Dublin Corporation made a compulsory purchase order under the Housing Act 1966 on 15 December 1967. Mr Murphy objected to this order and a public inquiry into this and other objections was held in April 1968. In due course the inspector who presided over this inquiry furnished a written report of the proceedings to the Minister who confirmed the Corporation's compulsory purchase order.

Subsequently, Mr Murphy brought an action in the High Court challenging the validity both of the compulsory purchase order made by Dublin Corporation and the Minister's confirmation thereof. Either party to such an action is entitled, if necessary by way of motion to the court, to force the other to disclose the existence of all relevant documentation in his possession and to make this available to the moving party for copying and scrutiny. The Minister disclosed the existence of the inspector's report in response to such an application taken by Mr Murphy but claimed for several reasons to be described later, to be entitled to withhold it. This claim is known as a claim of privilege. Mr Murphy suspected correctly that the report was favourable to him in as far as it recommended that the Minister should not confirm the compulsory purchase order over his lands and challenged the Minister's claim to privilege on this point and was ultimately successful in the Supreme Court. This case is shortly referred to as *Murphy No. 1.*

Armed, thus, with the inspector's report, Mr Murphy felt himself in a position to challenge the Minister's confirmation of the compulsory purchase order, relying largely on the inspector's recommendation and also on the evidence supporting that recommendation and contained in the report. In this action which was also taken to the Supreme Court, Mr Murphy failed and, accordingly, the local authority was entitled to acquire his lands compulsorily, subject, of course, to the payment of compensation. This second action is referred to shortly as *Murphy No. 2.*

The matter duly came before an arbitrator for the purpose of assessing compensation and arising out of this hearing a case was stated to the High Court for the determination of two questions. Dublin Corporation had served two notices to treat,[2] and as there was a material difference in land prices on the dates of the two notices to treat, a question arose as to which one was the operative notice in Mr Murphy's case. This was one of two questions raised in the case stated to the High Court.

The second was whether the arbitrator was entitled to have regard to the transcript of the proceedings at the public local inquiry into the original objections to Dublin Corporation's compulsory purchase order. This transcript had come to hand by reason of Mr Murphy's success in *Murphy No. 1* and disclosed that the Minister had been prepared to waive the provisions of the Dublin County Council development plan insofar as this plan had reserved as agricultural land some of the lands being acquired from Mr Murphy. The effect of this waiver was to increase the attractiveness to a purchaser and hence the market value of these lands. It had already been established by the Supreme Court[3] that the primary measure of compensation to be paid by an acquiring authority in such cases is the open market value of the lands. Because this value would be affected by a determination of the question whether or not the arbitrator was entitled to have regard to the report the matter was also referred to the High Court in the case stated.

In the event it was decided by the Supreme Court[4] that the first notice to treat was the operative one[5] and that the arbitrator was not entitled to have regard to the contents of the transcript of evidence of the proceedings before the inspector. This case is shortly referred to as *Murphy No. 3.*

It will be seen that three important developments have taken place in this field since 1970; the whole question of ministerial privilege in civil[6] matters has been considered; the role of the Minister when deciding whether or not to confirm a compulsory purchase order has been defined; and the rules determining the level of compensation payable to a compulsory vendor have been clarified. These topics will now be dealt with in more detail.

Ministerial Privilege

In times of civil disturbance and particularly in times of war, it is often felt necessary by governments to pass laws and claim privileges which would in times of peace and good order be considered contrary to the best interests of justice, having regard to the right balance which must be maintained between the public interest on the one side and on the other that of the individual.

In 1939 an English submarine 'The Thetis' sank during her trials, with the loss of ninety-nine men. Some of the men's dependants brought actions for negligence against the contractors who had built the submarine.[7] During the proceedings the plaintiffs called on the contractors to produce relevant material, including their contract with the Admiralty, which included specifications for the hull and machinery of the 'The Thetis' and also for salvage reports made after the accident.

The First Lord of the Admiralty swore an affidavit to the effect that disclosure would be against the public interest. The House of Lords held that this affidavit could not be questioned and in the result the plaintiffs lost their case. In fact, it was disclosed after the war that the class of submarine to which the 'The Thetis' belonged, carried a new type of torpedo tube which was still secret in 1942.

Clearly in this case production of the specifications and reports required would have been injurious to the public interest and the First Lord's affidavit reflected an entirely reasonable point of view. Unfortunately the decision of the House of Lords took the form of a sweeping rule that the courts could not question a claim of Crown Privilege made in proper form regardless of the nature and contents of the material sought to be discovered. In effect, the court thereby handed over to the administration the right to determine the question whether or not a document should be produced. Given this encouragement the practice grew up of claiming privilege for documents on the mere ground that they belonged to a certain class which should be kept secret in the public interest.

This decision was followed in Ireland in the case of *Attorney General* v. *Simpson.*[8] In that case, which arose out of a prosecution for showing for gain an indecent and profane performance at a Dublin theatre, it was sought on behalf of the defendant to have produced a report made by a garda witness who had attended one of the performances in question and further, to have a second garda witness say what were the instructions given him by his superior officer who directed him to go and see the play.

It was held by the High Court that this evidence was privileged because it consisted of communications between members of the Garda Síochána in the course of their duties and, as such, belonged to a class of evidence, the admission of which would be against the public interest. Davitt P., however, delivered a dissenting judgment which was referred to by Walsh J. in his judgment in *Murphy No. 1* in the following terms:

> I have considered the exhaustive judgment of Davitt P. in *Attorney General* v. *Simpson*. In so far as he deals with the present point, he came to the conclusion at p. 128 of the report that the decision of the House of Lords in *Duncan* v. *Cammel Laird & Co. Ltd.* represented in general what had been accepted in this country as the law upon the matter of privilege. It is to be noted that in *Conway* v. *Rimmer*[9] the House of Lords departed from the view taken in *Duncan* v. *Cammel Laird & Co. Ltd.* In my view, the principles enunciated in support of our law being in accord with the latter decision were based on considerations which are inconsistent with the supremacy of the judicial power under the Constitution in the administration of justice. Those principles were first formulated when such constitutional supremacy did not exist; they do not now prevail.[10]

The documents in question in the case of *Conway* v. *Rimmer* referred to in this passage were the reports concerning a probationer police constable made by his superiors. The constable had been prosecuted by the police for theft of an electric torch and decisively acquitted.

He sued the prosecutor for damages for malicious prosecution and applied to the court for the production of five reports about himself which were in the records of the police and which were both relevant and important to his case as evidence on the question of malice.

The Home Secretary claimed that confidential police records belonged to a class of document, the production of which would be injurious to the public interest. The House of Lords rejected this claim and made it clear that such claims were being made too often and without due regard for the interests of the individual litigant.

The point here was that the court reserved for itself the power to decide the issue where a conflict of interest existed between the public good and that of the individual, and rejected the right of the Home Secretary to make this decision himself.

Indeed, Kenny J. who decided *Murphy No. 1* in the High Court, accepted that *Conway* v. *Rimmer* and a Scottish case *Glasgow Corporation* v. *Central Land Board*[11] correctly stated the law in Ireland. As he said in his judgment at p. 226:

> They established that a Government Minister has no absolute right to withhold production of any documents, and that in every case the issue whether the documents should be made available to the other parties to the litigation should be decided by the court which has jurisdiction to require production of the documents to it for inspection.

However, Kenny J. went on to say that when a Minister certifies that the production of a specific document which he has considered would be against the public interest, the court should accept his view unless it is shown not to have been formed in good faith, is one which no reasonable Minister could take or is based on a misunderstanding of the issues in the case. Since none of these provisos applied, Kenny J. upheld the claim of privilege.

On this specific point Walsh J. disagreed with the trial judge and expressed the view that the onus lies on the Minister to make the case for non-production. Such a case had not been made for the non-production of the document concerned and in that event the learned trial judge ought to have directed production of the document, at least for his own inspection, when he could then decide the matter.[12]

The foregoing views and decisions relate to a claim of executive privilege from production of a document brought into being in the course of the carrying out of the executive functions of the state.

In the last pages[13] of his judgment in *Murphy No. 1* however, Walsh J. distinguished between the executive powers of a government and the judicial function which the Minister carried out when acting as the adjudicating authority upon a dispute which arises between the owner of land which is made the subject of a compulsory purchase order and the local authority making such an order.

He made clear that the latter function is not an executive power of the state; rather the holder of the office of the Minister for Local Government is the person designated to perform this function. The function might just as easily have been assigned to the chairman of Córas Iompair Éireann and if it had been there could be no question of such a person being granted the executive privilege of non-production of the inspector's report. Equally, the

Act had not required that the person appointed to conduct the inquiry should be a civil servant and the fact that such a person had been appointed did not entitle the Minister to confer upon the function the privileges or protections, if any, which hedge a civil servant in the business of the state assigned to him.[14]

The Role of the Inspector

In the last two paragraphs of his judgment in *Murphy No. 1*, Walsh J. set out the role of the inspector in such cases and also that of the Minister. Because these two paragraphs provided the basis for subsequent successful challenges to confirmed compulsory purchase orders in the courts they are now set out in full:

> In this context it is necessary to examine the precise function of the inspector in this role. By Statute the Minister is the one who has to decide the matter — not the inspector. In doing so, the Minister must act judicially and within the bounds of constitutional justice. No direct assistance is obtainable from the Statute as to the precise functions of the inspector or of his powers. It is clear, however, that in so far as the conduct of the inquiry is concerned he is acting as recorder for the Minister. He may regulate the procedure within the permissible limits over which he presides. In as much as he is there for the purpose of reporting to the Minister, the inspector's function is to convey to the Minister, if not a verbatim account of the entire of the proceedings before him, at least a fair and accurate account of what transpired and one which gives accurately to the Minister the evidence and the submissions of each party because it is upon this material that the Minister must make his decision and on no other. The inspector has no advisory function nor has he any function to arrive at a preliminary judgment which may or may not be confirmed or varied by the Minister. If the inspector's report takes the form of a document then it must contain an account of all the essentials of the proceedings over which he presided. In my view, it is not part of his function to arrive at any conclusion. If the Minister is influenced in his decision by the opinions of the inspector or the conclusions of the inspector, the Minister's decision will be open to review. It may be quashed and set aside if shown to be based on materials other than those disclosed at the public hearing.
>
> In my view, in the exercise of the function which he was performing in this case, it was not open to the Minister to refuse to produce the inspector's report on the ground that it is a document for which the executive privilege of non-production is available, if granted by the court; I refer to "Executive privilege" for want of a better term. It follows that it was not open to the High Court to refuse to order production of the document in question on the grounds given by Mr Justice Kenny. I would allow the appeal.

The practical significance of these general observations became apparent in the case of *Killiney and Ballybrack Development*

Association Ltd. v. *the Minister for Local Government and Templefin Estates Ltd.* decided by Finlay P. in the High Court[15] in which the fact that the report of an inspector who presided over an oral planning appeal contained an account of a visit made to the development site by the inspector in person which was not referred to at the oral hearing was sufficient in the circumstances of the case to invalidate the Minister's confirmation of the planning permission because it was, in the words of Walsh J. quoted above '. . . based on materials other than those disclosed at the public hearing'.

In this case, which involved an application by a developer for a housing development, the capacity of the sewage disposal facilities to deal with the existing situation let alone that which would be created by the proposed development was left in a state of doubt because one witness stated that there were signs of sewage, rubbish, etc. along the beach in question and that there were also signs of raw sewage, while a second stated that on a number of visits there was no sign of raw sewage. Accordingly, a direct conflict of fact on this important question had arisen and the trial judge commented[16] that it was possible to construe the inspector's account of his own visit and observations in the area as taking sides as between the two conflicting witnesses. In these circumstances therefore, the material included in the inspector's report which had not been disclosed at the public hearing was of a character capable of influencing the Minister and for this reason and 'because of the absence of any reasons in the decision of the Minister indicating upon what evidence he relied and upon what evidence he did not rely'[17] the trial judge held that the inclusion invalidated the Minister's confirmation.

It is important to note that the word used by Walsh J. in the *Murphy No. 1* case was that an order *may* be quashed. Invalidity is not an automatic consequence of the inclusion of material not disclosed at the public hearing in the inspector's report; invalidity arises only when the court in the exercise of its discretion declares the confirmation to be invalid.

The judgment of Finlay P. in the *Ballybrack* case is also of note because in it the judge specifically observed that he could find no distinction in principle between the procedure for the conduct of public oral inquiries under the Housing Acts and that for the conduct of appeals under the Planning Act.

Each concerns and vitally affects the property rights of citizens; each is a decision imposed upon a Minister of State[18] who does not himself hold the inquiry. Each provides for an inquiry, however, to be held by a person nominated by him with a duty to report to him. Although the Planning Acts and the Regulations made under it do provide powers for the inspector, it cannot be said on my reading of them that they define his precise functions nor is there any suggestion that he has any advisory functions.

I therefore, conclude that the test which I must apply to the issues in this case is the test laid down by Mr Justice Walsh in the portion of his judgment which I have just above quoted.[19]

The principles with which the courts will test the validity of decisions arrived at under the two procedures were therefore, the same until by section 23 of the Planning Act 1976 the inspector was required to include a recommendation.[20] This did not mean, however, that the Housing and Planning Acts were to be regarded as a single code. On the contrary, in delivering the judgment of the Supreme Court in *Murphy No. 2,* Henchy J. specifically rejected this proposition:

> The two Acts in question are not *in pari materia.* They lack a common subject matter or purpose. So it would be a breach of a fundamental rule of interpretation to treat them as a statutory whole.[21]

The point arose again in similar circumstances in the case of *Susan Geraghty* v. *The Minister for Local Government,*[22] where it is dealt with by Walsh J. as follows:

> In *Murphy's* case the Court also expressed the view that if the Minister was influenced in his decision by the opinions of the inspector or the conclusions of the inspector, the Minister's decision would be open to review. At p. 239 of the report, the court went on to say — "It may be quashed and set aside if it is shown to be based on materials other than those disclosed at the public hearing". The meaning of this is quite clear. It is the Minister's business and duty to arrive at the decision and to arrive at it upon a proper consideration of the materials which the parties had an opportunity to deal with at the inquiry. If the Minister arrives at a particular decision or conclusion because it is the one voiced by the inspector as one he, the Minister, ought to come to, then the Minister has failed to exercise his statutory function and his decision will be quashed.

The views of Henchy J. in the same case while differing in some respects from those of the majority of the court were to the same effect on the main point:

> I conclude that the appointed person *must* include in his report a fair and accurate summary of the evidence and submissions together with his findings of fact, and that he *may* include observations, inferences, submissions and recommendations limited to what took place at the hearing.[23]

It was pointed out by the then Chief Justice Ó Dálaigh, in the case of *In re Haughey*:[24]

> Article 40, Section 3 of the Constitution is a guarantee to the citizen of basic fairness of procedures. The Constitution guarantees such fairness, and it is the duty of the court to underline that the words of Article 40, Section 3 are not political shibboleths but provide a positive protection for the citizen and his good name.

It would seem therefore, that not only is there general judicial agreement that the procedures for public hearings under the Housing and Planning Acts will be reviewed by the courts by reference to the same principles, but also that these principles or ones similar to them are the operative ones whenever a decision by 'any body or person having legal authority to determine questions affecting the rights of subjects and having the duty to act judicially' is under review.[25]

Role of the Minister

It is clear from the foregoing that the Minister (and now, the Planning Board in most planning appeals) is the person required by the Oireachtas to make the decision in these cases. These tribunals are not, however, in the same position as a judge trying a contest at arm's length between two parties. This point was made by Ó Caoimh P. (as he then was) in his judgment in the *Murphy No. 2* case:[26]

> The inspector seems to me to have made a mistake in his approach to this matter when he was preparing his report and the plaintiff and his advisers seemed to me to make the same mistake. They appeared to treat this . . . as a contest between the Corporation and the owner as to who should be allowed to build houses on these lands. The Statute does not entrust to the Minister the decision of any such contest at all. The Statute entrusts to the Minister the decision to affirm, with or without modification, or not to affirm the compulsory purchase order and in order to consider what he has to do one has to look back to the reason for the compulsory purchase order at all.[27]

If there is a conflict of evidence on any point therefore, the Minister is not in the position of a judge who has to weigh one set of evidence against another and to determine on balance which is more probable; rather he is entitled to act on any evidence correctly before him provided it is not of so flimsy a character that it would be unreasonable or perverse to rely on it.

The same judge made the point in other words in the case of *An Taisce* v. *Dublin Corporation*[28] in which the plaintiff claimed an injunction to restrain the defendants from dumping refuse on a portion of the Bull Island and a declaration that it was their duty under section 22 sub-section (1) of the Local Government (Planning and Development) Act 1963 to take steps to secure the objectives contained in the development plan for the area of which they were the planning authority.

Again in this case, there was a conflict of technical evidence which the plaintiffs asked the court to resolve in their favour. In the course of his judgment Ó Caoimh P. observed as follows:

> It seems to me that it is for the Corporation to determine to what extent the trippers are to be favoured and the bird-watchers treated less favourably . . . and it is not for the court to determine the precise area of the Bull Island which should be retained as a bird sanctuary or the precise area of the Bull Island which should be made available as an amenity for the ordinary city dweller. This is a function of the planning authority and not of the court.[29]

And again at p. 5:

> It seems to me that it is sufficient if there is a body of expert opinion on which the Corporation are entitled to rely and which is favourable to the view put forward by them.

Apart therefore, from a gross departure from the provisions of the development plan, any reasonable scheme undertaken by the planning authority and supported by the opinions of a body of experts, even if such opinion has not been proved to be the preponderant expert view and providing that such a scheme was not a gross departure from the plan, would not be disturbed by the court. It is no part of the function of the court to replace a decision of a planning authority by the decision which it would have taken in the light of the evidence before such authority in the manner of an appellate court dealing afresh with all the evidence.[30] Rather the concern of the court is to see that the authority acted within the power conferred on it by the Oireachtas and once this has been established the wisdom of the deciding authority prevails. It is to the planning authority or the acquiring authority or the Minister or Board on appeal and not to the courts that the Oireachtas has entrusted the making of such decisions and once they are taken under the correct jurisdiction they will not be invalidated by the courts.

As has been seen, the courts will certainly infer, either by reference to the Acts in question or to the Constitution or both that such jurisdiction is limited by the rules of natural and constitutional justice which guarantees basic fairness of procedures. Accordingly, where a court finds that a refusal to grant planning permission, either *de novo* or on appeal, was invalid — as happened in the case of *Susan Geraghty* v. *The Minister for Local Government* — it does not grant the planning permission but directs a fresh hearing of the appeal in accordance with the provisions of the Planning Acts.[31] In the course of his judgment in *Geraghty's* case, Walsh J. said:

> In cases of inquiries for which no formal procedure is laid down, the principles enunciated by this court in *East Donegal Co-operative Livestock Mart Ltd.* v. *Attorney General*[32] would be applicable . . .

These principles are set out at pp. 343-344 of the report of that case as follows:

> All the powers granted to the Minister by section 3 (of the Livestock Marts Act, 1967 (No. 20 of 1967), which was under challenge for repugnance to the Constitution in this case) which are prefaced or followed by the words "at his discretion" or "as he shall think proper" or "if he so thinks fit" are powers which may be exercised only within the boundaries of the stated objects of the Act; they are powers which cast upon the Minister the duty of acting fairly and judicially in accordance with the principles of constitutional justice, and they do not give him an absolute or unqualified or an arbitrary power to grant or refuse at his will. Therefore, he is required to consider every case upon its own merits, to hear what the applicant or the licensee (as the case may be) has to say, and to give the latter an opportunity to deal with whatever case may be thought to exist against the granting of a licence or for the refusal of a licence or for the attaching of conditions, or for the amendment or revocation of conditions which have already attached, as the case may be.

In the case *McDonald* v. *Bord na gCon* the same judge had pointed out that the concept of constitutional justice comprises more than is embraced in the two principles or precepts which constitute natural justice as a recognised legal concept.[33] Whether a plaintiff can join the Minister as defendant to proceedings attacking the validity of a compulsory purchase order depends on whether any charge is made against him;[34] he may not be joined solely in order to force him to discover a copy of the inspector's report.[35]

CHAPTER THREE

Compulsory Acquisition: Scope of the Power

No local authority or other body has power compulsorily to acquire land without explicit authorisation by statute. The basic test therefore, of the scope of such power in any particular instance is to be found in the authorising statute. For example, section 76 of the Housing Act 1966 authorises a housing authority to acquire land compulsorily for the purposes of that Act by means of a compulsory purchase order made by the authority and confirmed by the Minister in accordance with the provisions contained in the Third Schedule of the Act. There are several limitations on this power which need be referred to only briefly. The power is conferred only on a housing authority; the land must be acquired only for the purposes of the Housing Act; it can be acquired only by means of a compulsory purchase order made by the housing authority, submitted to the Minister and confirmed by him in accordance with the Third Schedule to the Act.

The 'purposes' of the Act are to be found from a reading of the Act in accordance with the principles laid down in the *East Donegal Marts* case[1] and will include acquisition of land for satisfying the objectives set out for example at section 55 (3) of the Act which objectives include such matters as the elimination of over-crowding, the provision of adequate housing accommodation for persons who need it and are unable to provide it from their own resources, the provision of sites for building purposes, and the securing of the objectives contained in the development plant for the area of the acquiring authority.

In *Murphy No. 2,*[2] apart from the challenge to the validity of the order as confirmed, on the grounds that the evidence was insufficient, a second challenge was mounted to its validity on the following ground:

The compulsory purchase order, being in respect of land which the Corporation intended to acquire compulsorily for the purposes of the Act of 1966 and which was outside their functional area and within the func-

tional area of the County Council, was invalid because, in order to comply
with section 109 (2) of the Act of 1966, the Corporation should first
have entered into an agreement with the County Council providing that it
was the Corporation and not the County Council who would acquire the
land compulsorily.[3]

Section 109 of the Housing Act 1966 reads in part as follows:

(1) A housing authority may perform any of their functions under this
Act outside their functional area. (2) Where a housing authority intends
to perform a function in the functional area of another housing authority,
the authority by whom the function is intended to be performed and the
other authority may make and carry out an agreement in relation to the
function, and where an agreement is made under this section the parties
to the agreement may terminate it at any time if they so agree.

It was suggested by the plaintiff that the true interpretation
of this section is that before an authority performed any of its
functions outside its functional area, it was required to have
entered into an agreement with the authority in whose area such
exercise was to take place. In support of this reading it was argued
that the word 'may' should be read as 'shall' but Henchy J. having
noted that the word 'may' occurs seventeen times in Part VII
(the relevant part) of the Act and the word 'shall' occurs five times,
observed: 'In no instance does there appear to be a confusion of
one word for the other'.[4] Moreover, the section is silent as to when
the agreement is to be entered into so it would be open in accordance with the reasoning in *Tralee UDC* v. *McSweeney*[5] to argue
that an agreement entered into after the acquisition of the lands
was sufficient compliance with the sub-section, always supposing
that such agreement was necessary at all. A further difficulty was
that the agreement referred to was described simply as 'an agreement in relation to the function' and this was not necessarily an
agreement to perform the function.

In further support of the plaintiff's proposed reading of the sub-
section it was argued that in order to give a reasonable and legis-
latively harmonious effect to the section, sub-section 2 should
be construed as making a prior agreement a necessary pre-condition
to the exercise of the power conferred in sub-section 1 because
the proposals of the acquiring authority could be in contravention of the development plan of the planning authority in which
the lands were situate and that, accordingly, the Local Government (Planning and Development) Act 1963 should be read

together with the Housing Act 1966 so as to provide legislative harmony.[6] In rejecting this argument Henchy J., as already noted, observed that the two Acts in question were not *in pari materia*. He further observed that before any development could occur, the requisite permission under the Planning Act 1963 would have to be given by the Planning Authority for the area in which the lands were situate.

It is now established, therefore, that the compulsory purchase powers conferred on a housing authority under the Housing Act 1966 may be exercised outside the functional area of that authority and that the agreement referred to at section 109 (2) of the Housing Act 1966 is not a necessary pre-condition to such exercise. In the case of Dublin Corporation, for example, and indeed of any housing authority faced with a shortage of development land within its functional area, this clarification was of crucial importance.

A further attack on the validity of a compulsory purchase order made by Dublin Corporation over lands outside its functional area was made in the case of *Moran* v. *Corporation of Dublin.*[7]

In that case the plaintiff successfully argued in the High and Supreme Courts that the compulsory purchase order was invalidated because there was evidence to show that while the lands were being acquired by the defendants partly to carry out their own housing programme, they were also being acquired for the purpose of carrying out the housing programme of Dublin County Council.

During the 1960s it became clear by reason of the shortage of land within its functional area that Dublin Corporation would have to·build in the County. However, their power to acquire outside their functional area was limited.

By section 7 of the Housing of the Working Classes Act 1908 there was power to acquire land outside their functional area if they had the consent of the local authority in whose area the land was situate and of the Local Government Board.

By section 29 of the Housing (Amendment) Act 1952 the only consent necessary became that of the housing authority in whose area the lands were situate. A doubt existed, however, as to whether these provisions applied to compulsory acquisition outside the functional area of a housing authority and so section 109, referred to already, was included in the Housing Act 1966.

A further limitation on the acquisition powers of a local authority existed prior to 1946 when lands could be acquired only for immediate[8] use. Section 82 of the Local Government Act 1946 (which is still in force) extended the power to the acquisition by agreement of lands for use in the future, even though it had not been decided how or for which purpose the lands would be used. Further, by section 77 of the Housing Act 1966 the housing authority may be authorised to acquire compulsorily land not immediately required for housing purposes if the Minister is of the opinion that there is a reasonable expectation that the land will be required by the authority in the future in order to attain any of the objectives mentioned in section 55, sub-section 3 of the Act.

These statutory developments were reviewed by Kenny J. in his judgment in *Moran's* case[9] the effect of which developments he summed up as follows:

> The result is that since 1966, a local authority which is a housing authority may acquire land outside their functional area compulsorily without the consent of the local authority in whose area the lands are situate and for future use even if that has not been specifically determined.

At the public local inquiry into the objections to the making of the compulsory purchase order in this case there was evidence that the defendants were acquiring the lands partly for the purposes of providing houses on them to satisfy the needs of the Dublin County Council. Kenny J. held that this invalidated the order and observed:

> That a housing authority may acquire lands inside or outside their area to satisfy the needs of their functional area only seems to me a clear inference from section 55 sub-section 1 of the Act of 1966 which reads:
> "It shall be the duty of a housing authority, within such period after the commencement of this section as may be specified by the Minister and thereafter either at least once in every five years or at such intervals, being less than five years, as the Minister may direct from time to time, to prepare and adopt a programme (in this Act referred to as a building programme) setting out the works which they propose to undertake having regard to the housing needs of their functional area." There is no provision in the Act of 1966 which authorises local authorities to undertake a joint housing programme and there is nothing which allows one housing authority to acquire lands for the housing programme of another. A housing authority has power only to acquire lands under the Act of 1966 to satisfy their housing needs and not those of another authority. Section 110 authorises a housing authority to establish a joint committee with another housing authority for purposes connected with the functions under

this Act which are common to both parties to the agreement but this does not mean that two housing authorities may jointly acquire lands compulsorily . . . It follows that the Minister should have refused to confirm the compulsory purchase order . . .[10]

The plaintiffs were, accordingly, successful in the High Court on this point and this position was upheld in the Supreme Court and an order was made quashing the compulsory purchase order.

A second point made by the plaintiffs in this case did not meet with the approval of the trial judge. This point was that the acquiring authority should have obtained planning permission.

The argument here was that unless such permission is shown to have been granted, the Minister might in the future find himself required to decide a planning appeal against a development permission relating to the very lands in respect of which he had himself confirmed a compulsory purchase order. This, the argument runs, would put him in a position in which he could not be impartial.

In dealing with this argument Kenny J. was of the view that the Minister in such circumstances would not be prevented from deciding such an appeal in an impartial way. He also found a telling answer to the argument in section 77 of the 1966 Act under which lands not immediately required for the purposes of the Act can be compulsorily acquired if the Minister is of the opinion that there is a reasonable expectation that they will be required for such purposes in the future:

> If a local authority decides to acquire lands because they will be required in the future, it would be impossible to prepare an application for planning permission because this must be stated with considerable detail. The housing authority may not know which of the objectives in section 55, sub-section 3 they will ultimately decide to attain by acquiring the lands. Moreover, planning permission (as distinct from outline planning permission) postulates that services are available for the houses or buildings which will be erected on the lands and in the case of the acquisition of lands for future use, these services will not in most cases be available at the time when the compulsory purchase order is made.[11]

A housing authority therefore has no power to acquire lands compulsorily for the housing needs of another housing authority even if such lands are included in a compulsory purchase order which also includes lands which will be required for their own housing needs.

In the case of *Russell* v. *Minister for Local Government*[12] a compulsory purchase order was quashed by order of the High Court on the ground that the acquiring authority had no building programme which they were obliged to prepare by virtue of section 55 of the Housing Act 1966. The kernel of the judgment of Parke J. is contained in the following passage:

> Section 76 of the Act enables a housing authority to acquire land only for the purposes of the Act. In this case, the housing authorities say that they are acquiring land to satisfy their housing needs, but section 55 says that the housing needs of a housing authority must be defined in a way that is strictly controlled by the section. It is difficult to see how a housing authority can satisfy those needs when it has failed to comply with section 55. In those circumstances, a housing authority would be in a position that it had no needs to satisfy as envisaged by the Act.

The trial judge had taken the view that because the Minister had to be of the opinion that there was a reasonable expectation that land would be required for the purpose of the Act when section 77 (which deals with future needs) was invoked that in effect he could only arrive at that opinion if he had regard to the building programme prepared under section 55 and that, if there was no such programme, he could not reach that conclusion. If the existence of a building programme is a necessary pre-condition to the exercise of the powers of a housing authority under section 77, this was also true in relation to section 76 which was the section involved in the case at the hearing.

The defendants successfully appealed to the Supreme Court and in delivering the judgment to that court, Walsh J. took the view that while the existence of a building programme would enable the Minister to form a much clearer idea of the foreseeable needs of the housing authority in the future, it did not follow that given the proper evidence he could not form an opinion as to the reasonable expectation concerning the future in the absence of such a programme.[13] Sections 76 and 77 of the Act could not be read as being dependent on the pre-existence of a building programme,[14] and there was nothing in section 76 taken independently of section 77 which made the existence of a building programme a condition precedent to the exercise of the power under the section.[15] Accordingly, while the failure of a housing authority to prepare a building programme may put them in breach of their statutory duty under section 55,[16] such failure does not invalidate the exercise by the authority of its acquisition powers under section 76 or 77.

Compensation

The basic provision regulating the assessment of compensation for land compulsorily acquired in this country is section 2 of the Acquisition of Land (Assessment of Compensation) Act 1919, which sets out six rules[17] of which rule 2 is the most important and reads as follows:

> The value of land shall, subject as hereinafter provided, be taken to be the amount which the land if sold in the open market by a willing seller might be expected to realise; provided always that the arbitrator shall be entitled to consider all returns and assessments of capital value for taxation made or acquiesced in by the claimant.

By section 69 of the Local Government (Planning and Development) Act 1963, ten further rules (numbered 7 to 16) were added and are to be found in the Fourth Schedule to that Act. Of these, rule 13 provides as follows:

> No account shall be taken of (a) the existence of proposals for development of the land or any other land by a local authority, or (b) the possibility or probability of the land or other land becoming subject to a scheme of development undertaken by a local authority.

The leading Irish case on the application of these rules is *In re Deansrath Investments*.[18] In this case it was argued on behalf of the acquiring authority that the effect of rule 13 was that all potential uses of the lands, whether by a local authority or a private developer, were to be disregarded by the arbitrator in assessing compensation. The use of the land prior to the acquisition would, according to this argument, have been the sole basis for valuation. In other words, if the lands had been used as agricultural land prior to the acquisition, then this use and not the likelihood that in the future they would be used for housing development was to be the criterion for assessing compensation. This argument was rejected in a case stated to the High Court by Pringle J. and on appeal in turn by Budd J. delivering the judgment of the Supreme Court. In the absence of Irish authority dealing with the principles to be applied in giving effect to section 2 of the Act of 1919, both judges concluded that the same principles as had been laid down in a series of English decisions dealing with the construction of similar legislation and rules should apply in this country.

In the first of these decisions Lord Justice Fletcher Moulton in the case of *Lucas* v. *Chesterfield Gas and Water Board*[19] said:

The owner receives for the lands he gives up their equivalent, i.e., that which they were worth to him in money. His property is, therefore, not diminished in amount, but to that extent it is compulsorily changed in form. But the equivalent is estimated on the value to him, and not on the value to the purchaser, and hence it has from the first been recognised as an absolute rule that this value is to be estimated as it stood before the grant of the compulsory power. The owner is only to receive compensation based upon the market value of his lands as they stood before the scheme was authorised by which they are put into public uses. Subject to that he is entitled to be paid the full price for his lands, and any and every element of value which they possess must be taken into consideration in so far as they increase the value to him.

This passage together with an approving passage taken from Lord Dunedin giving the advice of the Privy Council in the case of *Cedars Rapids Manufacturing and Power Company* v. *Lacarte*[20] is cited with approval and relied upon by Budd J. in his judgment, and it is also noted that while these two cases were decided before the passing of the 1919 Act the same principles were applied in a number of cases decided in which section 2 of that Act was the governing section.

The point was further clarified in the case of *Pointe Gourde Quarrying and Transport Co. Ltd.* v. *Sub-Intendent of Crown Lands*[21] where it was stated by Lord McDermott that 'compensation for the compulsory purchase of land cannot include an increase in value which is entirely due to the scheme underlying the acquisition.'[22]

The principle established by these English authorities, namely, that in assessing compensation for the compulsory acquisition of land no account is to be taken of an increase in the value of that land or of other land due entirely to the scheme underlying the acquisition in question was adopted in a modified form in rule 13 which is to be found in the Fourth Schedule to the Planning Act 1963 and which reads:

No account shall be taken of:
(a) the existence of proposals for the development of land or any other land by a local authority, or
(b) the possibility or probability of the land or other land becoming subject to a scheme of development undertaken by a local authority.

As was pointed out by Budd J. in the *Deansrath* case, our legislation has gone further than the *Pointe Gourde* decision because rule 13(b) provides not only that existing proposals for development by a local authority must be disregarded but further that no account must be taken of the possibility or probability that the acquired land or other land may become subject to a scheme of such development.

However, rule 13 when construed in its proper context must be read merely as a restriction of the basic rule 2 as set out in section 2 of the 1919 Act already referred to. The rule is therefore, in effect, an addition to the list of specific items to which regard shall not be had when assessing compensation; in the *Deansrath* case it was of pivotal importance that this rule is concerned only with the proposals (existing or future) for development by a *local authority:*

> There is nothing in the rule which could be said to prohibit in any way the taking into consideration, for the purpose of the assessment of value, proposals for development or the possibility or probability of development by any person or body other than a local authority. . . The only conclusion to be drawn from the wording and draftsmanship of the rule is that it was quite open to the arbitrator, in sq far as Rule 13 is concerned, to take into consideration the potential development value of the lands by any person or body other than a local authority. If the legislature had intended that the possibility of private development was not to be considered or that the value of lands was to be confined to its value as it was used on the date of the notice to treat, it would assuredly have said so. The legislature has not done so and the market value is left as the ruling factor, subject only to the restrictions imposed by Rule 13 and by any subsequent rules.[23]

A distinction is made in this passage between the value of the land as it was used on the date of the notice to treat and the market value. The market value would include 'every element of value which they possess . . . in so far as they increase the value to him'[24] and the potential development possibilities of the land are obviously one of the elements of such value.[25]

In a further comment, on rule 13, Budd J. suggested that the rule was designed to prevent a compulsory vendor receiving an enhanced value for his lands owing to the expenditure of public money in their development.[26]

The issues in *Murphy No. 3* have already been indicated[27] and are stated thus in the judgment of Henchy J.:[28]

> The acquiring authority then served another notice to treat on the 10th May, 1974, thereby implying that they considered the one served on the 12th March, 1973, to have been invalidly served. When the matter came before the arbitrator to fix compensation for the compulsory acquisition, he stated a case for the High Court seeking a ruling on two questions:

(1) which of the two notices to treat served was the effective one? and
(2) was the arbitrator entitled to have regard to the transcript of the pro-
     ceedings at the local public inquiry held prior to the confirmation of
     the compulsory purchase order, for the purpose of assessing the
     potential value of the land?

The answer given in the High Court to the first question was that it was
the second notice to treat that was the effective one. The answer given to
the second question was that the arbitrator could have regard to the
transcript, but only "so far as it may indicate that in relation to a proposal by the acquiring authority to develop the land for residential purposes
the Minister was prepared to consent to a departure from the zoning of the
land for agricultural purposes".

The answer to the first of these questions turned on the issue
whether an application to the courts to quash a compulsory purchase order is 'determined'[29] after the High Court or Supreme
Court proceedings. This issue was dealt with by Henchy J., delivering the judgment of the Supreme Court as follows:

> In my opinion, that determination necessarily refers to a determination
> in the High Court. The only court referred to, expressly or by implica-
> tion, in section 78 is the High Court. Section 78(2) (a) empowers the
> High Court to make an interim order suspending the operation of a com-
> pulsory purchase order "until the final determination of the proceedings".
> But "final" there is used in contrast to "interim" and means simply the
> final determination of the application in the High Court. When "final"
> is used with reference to a judgment, it does not mean a judgment which
> is not open to appeal, but final as distinguished from interlocutory: per
> Cozens-Hardy L. J. in *Huntley* v. *Gaskell* (1905 2 Ch. 656 at p. 667).
> When "determination of the proceedings" is used in subs. (3) (b) it can have
> no wider connotation than "final determination" has in subs. (3) (a),
> namely, final determination in the High Court.[30]

Henchy J. also pointed out that if this were not the case then
where an application was unsuccessfully brought in the High
Court an authority could not serve a notice to treat at least
until after the period for serving a notice of appeal to the Supreme
Court has run out. This would be to equate the phrase 'date of
determination' referred to in sub-section (3) (2) to a date fixed by
rules of court and would also give rise to an unworkable situation
if an acquiring authority validly served a notice to treat after the
period for appealing had expired and the claimant was then given
an extension of time within which to appeal. Since there was no
power in the Act to withdraw a valid notice to treat and equally
none to serve a second one a valid notice to treat could not be

served in compliance with the Act in such a case after the determination of the appeal to the Supreme Court.[31]

Dealing with the second question, Henchy J. pointed out that the short answer to this was that it was not proper for an arbitrator to rely on evidence given in other proceedings for the purpose of proving facts relevant in the arbitration and further, that the fact that the transcript was available at all in the present case was simply an accident of litigation due to the success of the plaintiff in *Murphy No. 1.*[32]

The judge then went on[33] to point out that for the arbitrator to conclude that because the Minister might be prepared to vary a development plan for the purpose of accommodating a local authority housing scheme he would therefore be prepared to do the same in the case of a private scheme would be erroneous.

Finally, the most fundamental reason why the arbitrator may not have regard to the Minister's confirmation of the compulsory purchase order was that he was debarred by statute from doing so. Henchy J. quoted rule 13[34] which precludes, *inter alia,* the taking account of the existence of proposals for the development of the land or any other land by a local authority and proceeded to explain the policy lying behind this rule in the following passage:

> The reason for that restriction is plain. It is to ensure that the acquiring authority will not have to pay more for the land than would an ordinary purchaser if a local authority development were not overshadowing this or other land. In other words, local authority interest — actually existing or even possibly impending — in land, for development purpose, is not allowed to trigger off increased land values in compulsory acquisitions. Local authorities are assured that they will not inflate land values against themselves if they are assiduous in carrying out, or even in considering carrying out, the development of land. This, if one may say so, is a commonsense rule, for if it did not apply, the compulsory acquisition of land for housing and other socially desirable purposes would be cramped by the consequence that from the time a local authority showed an interest in developing a particular piece of land, they would as a result not only have to pay a higher price for the land than it was worth before they cast their eye on it, but as well they would have to pay a consequentially inflated price for any other land which could be said to be enhanced in value by the proposed development. Compulsory acquisition could be effected only on prohibitively high terms. This would not be in the public interest.[35]

CHAPTER FOUR

Planning: Role of the Planning Authority

The law relating to planning and development in Ireland is governed by the Local Government (Planning and Development) Acts of 1963 and 1976 referred to in this and the following chapters as the 1963 Act and the 1976 Act respectively.

The 1963 Act replaced the Town and Regional Planning Acts, 1934 and 1939, and adopted many of the features of those Acts. The main difference effected by the 1963 Act was that each planning authority was obliged[1] by section 19 to make a development plan which was to be a written statement containing certain minimum planning objectives to be accompanied by a plan illustrating these. These development plans form the framework against which decisions are taken by planning authorities and on appeal by the Planning Board[2] (An Bord Pleanála) which came into existence on January 1 1977.

Under the Planning Acts planning authorities are also given wide powers in relation to commercial, industrial and community development over and above the preparation of development plans and the public is given a right to participate[3] in the preparation of development plans and also the determination[4] of any planning decision.

Provision is also made[5] for the payment of compensation by planning authorities to applicants for planning permission in certain cases and in such cases the primary measure of assessment is the market value of the land. In the event of disagreement the amount of compensation is as appropriate to a compulsory acquisition.[6]

Development by Planning Authorities
Part 7 of the 1963 Act comprising sections 74-79 confers on planning authorities extensive powers enabling them to secure the proper development of land in their areas. Land already vested in planning authorities otherwise than for the purposes of the 1963 Act may with the consent of the appropriate Minister be used by

31

them for the purposes of the Act.[7] Section 75 enables a planning authority to dispose of land held by them by way of sale, lease or exchange to facilitate the proper planning and development of their area. This section also enables a planning authority to make short leases of such land and provides that neither the Landlord and Tenant Acts nor the Rent Restrictions Acts shall apply to such leases. Provision is also made[8] for the extinction, with the approval of the Minister and after a public local enquiry, of a public right-of-way by a planning authority.

Section 77 enables a planning authority to 'develop or secure the development of land' and specifies particular instances of this general power such as, widening and improving roads, developing land near roads or bridges, providing areas in need with roads, services and other works, providing areas of convenient shape for development, securing and carrying out the development or renewal of obsolete areas, and securing the preservation of any view, physical feature, trees or sites of geological, ecological or archaeological interest or any flora or fauna subject to a conservation order.[9]

Further, a planning authority may provide sites for the establishment or re-location of industries, businesses, dwellings, offices, shops, schools, churches and other community facilities, and for factory buildings, office premises, shop premises, dwellings, amusement parks and other community services and any services considered ancillary to these items and a planning authority may maintain or manage any site or building, premises, dwelling, park, structure or service and may make any reasonable charges in respect thereof.[10]

It seems a planning authority has power compulsorily to acquire land for the purposes of the 1963 Act. In *Leinster Importing Co. Ltd* v. *Dublin County Council*[11] McWilliam J. held that the correct interpretation of section 11, Local Government (No. 2) Act, 1960 when construed with section 10, Local Government (Ireland) Act, 1898 was that the local planning authority could acquire land compulsorily under the new section 10, Local Government (No. 2) Act, 1960 as substituted by section 86, Housing Act, 1966.

In an earlier case of *Movie News Ltd.* v. *Galway County Council*[12] Kenny J., to whom neither section 11, Local Government (No. 2) Act, 1960 nor section 10, Local Government (Ireland)

Act, 1898 had been opened, held that there was nothing in the 1963 Act which authorises a local authority or a planning authority to acquire lands compulsorily for the purposes of that Act. In so finding the attention of the trial judge appears to have been directed primarily to section 10, Local Government (No. 2) Act 1960 and it was accepted on behalf of the local authority in the *Leinster Importing Co. Ltd.* case that this section does not give any power of acquisition for the purposes of the 1963 Act.

On 15 July 1977 an appeal by the local authority in the *Movie News* case came up for hearing in the Supreme Court.[13] When the appellant sought to extend the grounds of appeal to permit reliance on the statutory provisions successfully relied upon in the *Leinster Importing Co. Ltd.* case. The Supreme Court declined so to do on the grounds among others that if this point had been brought to the attention of the appeal court earlier the matter could have been sent back to the High Court. Henchy J. also indicated that the court did not intend to say what Acts should be cited in a compulsory purchase order.[14] Thus the High Court ruling stands in this case but it seems that if the local authority had relied on the statutory provisions successfully relied upon in the *Leinster Importing Co. Ltd.* case, they too would have been successful.[15]

The Meaning of Development
Unless a development was commenced before 1 October 1964 or unless it is exempted by the Planning Acts or the regulations made thereunder,[16] a permission must be obtained from the local planning authority before it can be undertaken.[17]

Development is defined by section 3 of the 1963 Act as 'the carrying out of any works, on, in, or under land or the making of any material change in the use of any structures or other land'. Two broad categories of development emerge, namely, construction works and change of use. Works include any act or operation of construction, excavation, demolition, extension, alteration, repair or renewal.[18] Change of use, however, does not include change of use incidental to the carrying out of works[19] but does include the use of a structure as two or more dwellings previously used as one, the use of land for the exhibition of advertisements or for caravan or camping sites and certain other specified purposes.[20] The general rule is that to constitute a material change of use the use must be substantially different from the previous use[21] but that an increase in the intensity of any use is not usually a material change.[22]

The Planning Acts make no explicit provision limiting the class of person who may apply for permission to develop land. Section 26 of the 1963 Act, which deals with permission for development, is concerned with the application and the conditions which may attach to it and not with the applicant. In relation to appeal section 26 (5) (a) of the 1963 Act refers to 'any person' who may appeal. In the case of *Frescati Estates Ltd.* v. *Marie Walker*[23] the following principles were laid down by the Supreme Court in deciding that an application for planning permission by a person with no interest in the land and made merely as part of a campaign to prevent another party from carrying out development was not made by an 'applicant' within the meaning of the 1963 Act:

> To sum up, while the intention of the Act is that persons with no legal interest (such as would be purchasers) may apply for development permission, the operation of the Act within the scope of its objects and the limits of constitutional requirements would be exceeded if the word "applicant" in the relevant sections is not given a restricted connotation. The extent of that restriction must be determined by the need to avoid unnecessary or vexatious applications, with consequent intrusion into property rights and demands on the statutory functions of planning authorities beyond what could reasonably be said to be required, in the interests of the common good, for proper planning and development.
>
> Applying that criterion I consider that an application for development permission, to be valid, must be made either by or with the approval of a person who is able to assert sufficient legal estate or interest to enable him to carry out the proposed development or so much of the proposed developement as relates to the property in question. There will thus be sufficient privity between the applicant (if he is not a person entitled) and the person entitled, to enable the applicant to be treated, for practical purposes as a person entitled.

The question of *locus standi* arose again in the context of an appeal in the case of *Andrew B. Law* v. *Minister for Local Government and Traditional Homes Ltd.*[24] in which Deale J. held *inter alia* that the mere fact that the plaintiff was not a party within the definition set out in the Appeals Regulations did not prevent him from challenging the validity of a planning permission confirmed by the Minister in the circumstance that he had a real interest in the appeal hearing.[25]

It will be seen therefore, that planning permission is required in a wide category of situations and because most of these will involve outlay it is a wise precaution to check with the relevant planning authority before embarking on development.[26]

Exempted Development
An exception to the foregoing will of course occur in the case of exempted developments. Section 4 of the 1963 Act lists some of the exempted developments, such as the use of land for some purposes of agriculture or forestry; several uses of land by local authorities; the carrying out of works of maintenance, improvement or other alteration of any structure which affect only the interior of the structure and do not materially affect the external appearance so as to render it out of keeping with neighbouring structures, and the use of any structure or land within the curtilage of a dwelling-house for a purpose incidental to the use of the structure as a dwelling-house.

Moreover, regulations made by virtue of sections 4 and 10 of the 1963 Act have greatly added to this list of exempted developments.

These regulations[27] make interesting reading. For example, no planning permission is necessary for the erection of a lighthouse while it is necessary to have planning permission to erect a television aerial if the same is more than six metres higher than the roof. Again, the extension of a dwelling-house by an addition to the rear provided that the height of the extension does not exceed that of the dwelling-house and the original floor area is not increased by more than eighteen square metres, is an exempted development.

Again, in these regulations several different types of advertisement are exempted[28] but generally subject to stringent conditions as to their size measured in square metres. For example, an advertisement exhibited at the entrance to any premises relating to any person, partnership or company separately carrying on a public service or a profession, business or trade at the premises is an exempted development provided it does not exceed 0.3 square metres in area and not more than one such advertisement is exhibited on the premises at each entrance to a road frontage.

A third category of such regulations refers to exempted rural developments; for example, the erection of ancillary farm buildings subject to dimensional and other limitations, and the temporary use of land by a scouting organisation for a summer camp (provided that the land shall not be used for such purposes for any period or periods exceeding thirty days in any year).[29] Finally, the use of land is divided into sixteen classes and a change of use from one to another of the uses specified within any of the classes is exempted development provided that it does not require the carrying out of works themselves requiring planning permission and provided the change of use would not contravene a condition attached to a permission given under the 1963 Act or be inconsistent therewith. Changes of use from one class to another require planning permission. For example, Class 2 consists of 'use as an office for any purposes'. Thus, a change of use of a premises from one kind of an office to another does not require planning permission. However, the change of use of a premises from use as an office to use as a light industrial building for any purposes (Class 3) would require permission. Some examples of the uses contained in the different classes are as follows: Class 10 comprises 'use as a resident- ial club, hotel providing sleeping accommodation, a guest house or a hostel'; Class 12 comprises 'use as a residential or boarding school or a residential college'; Class 15: 'use as a theatre, a cinema, a music hall, a concert hall'; Class 16: 'use as a skating rink, or a gymnasium, or for indoor games or sports (including boxing, wrestling and bowling)'.

The provisions relating to exempted developments are them- selves subject to several over-riding pre-conditions contained in article 11 of these regulations. For example, even if they would otherwise qualify for exemption the following developments are removed from this category: developments which contravene a condition attached to a permission under the Planning Acts or which are inconsistent with a use specified in such a permission; developments which constitute a traffic hazard or contravene building regulations or which involve building which would in- fringe a building line. The same applies to developments which restrict a view or amenity or interfere with a building singled out for preservation in a development plan or which affect an un- authorised structure or interfere with a public right-of-way. Again, several developments which would otherwise qualify for exemp- tion are excluded if they relate to land affected by a special amenity area order.

If a question arises as to what is development or exempted development the question may be referred to and decided by the Minister[30] by section 5 (1) of the 1963 Act and a further appeal lies from this decision to the High Court if taken within three months after the giving of the Minister's decision.[31]

The Development Plan

By section 19 of the 1963 Act, planning authorities are required to make plans indicating development objectives for their areas. As already indicated, the earlier Town Planning Acts enabled but did not require planning authorities to make such plans and, in fact, in no area did a planning scheme come into force under the earlier Acts.[32]

Under the 1963 Act each planning authority was obliged[1] to make such a plan within three years from 1 October 1964. This period could be and was extended by the Minister in particular cases.

Section 19 (2) of the 1963 Act provides that these development plans shall consist of a written statement and a plan indicating certain minimum development objectives for the area. These objectives include in urban areas the different zones (residential, commercial, industrial and so on) into which the land is to be divided; proposals for dealing with traffic needs with a view to convenience and safety of road users and pedestrians; proposals for the development and renewal of obsolete areas and for the development of amenities (which would include parks and buildings of historic or artistic interest); and in other areas objectives in relation to development of obsolete areas, amenities and the provision of water services.

Development plans may also include any or all of the objectives set out in the Third Schedule to the 1963 Act which contains a long list of such objectives.[33]

Provision is also made for the public advertisement of the making of draft development plans and for the making available of these plans for public inspection for a period of at least three months. Moreover, any objections or representations concerning the draft plans must be taken into consideration before the making of the development plan and any ratepayer making an objection is entitled to an opportunity to state his case before an appointee of the planning authority.[34] When the objections or representations have been considered the planning authority by passing the necessary resolution makes the development plan. The planning authority must publish notice of the making of the plan in at least one newspaper circulating in their area and in the *Iris*

Oifigiúil. This notice must state where and when a copy of the plan is available for public inspection.[35]

A planning authority must revise its plan at least once in every five years[36] and the Minister may require the planning authority to vary its plan[37] and he may also publish model plans for the guidance of planning authorities.[38]

Enforcement of Planning Control

In the case of any development of land which is neither exempted development nor development which has been commenced before 1 October 1964, and which has been carried out without the appropriate permission or in contravention of any conditions attached thereto, the planning authority may (and, if the Minister so directs, must) serve[39] within five years of the development being carried out or of the latest date specified for compliance with any condition an enforcement notice requiring discontinuance of the unauthorised use or the carrying out of works (including the removal or alteration of any structure). The notice shall specify a time within which compliance therewith must be completed and after that date the planning authority has power[40] to enter on the land and to carry out any works (including the removal or alteration of any structure) required by the enforcement notice and to recover the costs of such works from the owner of the land as a simple contract debt.[41] An owner of land who has failed to comply therewith shall be guilty of an offence[42] and shall be liable on summary conviction to a fine not exceeding £100 and if after conviction he does not as soon as practicable do everything in his power to secure compliance with the enforcement notice, he shall be guilty of a further offence and shall be liable on summary conviction to a fine not exceeding £20[43] for each day following the first conviction on which any of the requirements of the enforcement notice remains unfulfilled. These penalties have been increased to £250 and £50 respectively by section 38 of the 1976 Act.

Provision is also made[44] for the granting of permission to retain any structures on land made without the requisite permission under the 1963 Act and for the serving of an enforcement notice requiring the taking of steps to eliminate unauthorised development including for example the removal or alteration of structures or a change of use.[45]

Warning Notice

The explanatory memorandum to the 1976 Act lists as the second main purpose of this Act the strengthening of the provisions of the 1963 Act relating to unauthorised development. This strengthening is achieved in the following ways.

By section 26 of the 1976 Act, where it appears to a planning authority that unpermitted development is taking place or is about to take place or that unauthorised use is being made of land, the planning authority may serve on the owner of the land a warning notice directing that such development shall not take place or shall be discontinued forthwith as the case may be and directing the owner to take reasonable steps to comply with the notice. If any person knowingly fails to comply with the notice or assists another to breach it he shall be guilty of an offence and liable on summary conviction to a fine not exceeding £100 for each day of such breach or six months imprisonment or both.

Injunction

By section 27 it is provided that in the case of unauthorised development or use the High Court may, on the application[46] of the planning authority or any other person whether or not the person has an interest in the land, prohibit the continuance of the development or unauthorised use. Similar provisions are made with regard to a permitted development which is not being carried out in accordance with the permission. Breach of a High Court order would, of course, be a contempt of court.

Vesting Procedure

By section 25 where a planning permission has been given subject to a condition requiring the provision or maintenance of land as open space, a planning authority can serve upon the owner of that land a notice requiring him within a specified period not being less than two months to provide, level, plant, adapt or maintain it in a specified manner. If the owner fails to comply with this notice the planning authority may publish in a newspaper circulating in the district a further notice of their intention to acquire the land by a vesting order made under section 25 and this notice must give a minimum period of two months within which interested parties may appeal against the acquisition notice.

On appeal the Planning Board may either annul the acquisition notice or confirm it with or without modification (and in respect of all or part of the relevant lands) and insofar as the same is confirmed the planning authority may then make an order vesting the land in the planning authority for the estate and interest of the owner. This vesting order operates to vest the land with all its liabilities, including, for example, annuities payable to the Land Commission, in the local authority which is, then entitled to be registered as owner of the lands in accordance with the order. If the divested owner of the lands makes application for compensation and the same falls to be determined by arbitration under section 68 of the 1963 Act, the arbitrator must enter a nil award unless the owner can show the value of the land to which the relevant permission relates has not been and will not be recovered as a result of the development. Private open space is not affected by this section.

Withering

An important new element has been introduced by section 29 of the 1976 Act which provides for what is commonly known as the 'withering' of planning permission after a period of five years. By sub-sections (1) (a) and (b) this applies to the entire permission if it is not commenced within the five-year period and to so much of it as remains incomplete if it has been commenced. A saver is provided (sub-section (2) (a)) in the case of ancillary or incidental structures to the main development and (sub-section (b)) in the case of road surfaces and open spaces ancillary to completed development.

Provision is also made (sub-section (3)) for the granting of a waiver notice whereby a condition imposed on a planning permission which is not complied with within the five-year period may be waived and (sub-section (5)) for an appeal against a refusal to grant such a notice. Most importantly, by sub-section (9) a planning authority may 'as regards a particular permission by order extend or, from time to time, further extend the period referred to in sub-section (1) of this section by such additional period as the authority consider appropriate . . .' An appeal lies to the Circuit Court (sub-section 12) by any person aggrieved by the decision of a planning authority on an application for a development certificate which is a certificate stating that part of a development was completed within the five-year period in cases where a dispute has arisen on this point. No appeal from the decision of a planning authority to extend or not to extend the five-year period is provided and accordingly the only way such a challenge could be mounted would be on the grounds that the jurisdiction was improperly exercised.

CHAPTER FIVE

Planning: Role of the Developer

Planning Permission

The general obligation on the developer to obtain planning permission when the development in question is neither exempted nor commenced before 1 October 1964 is contained in section 24 of the 1963 Act and a general prohibition against carrying out any development except in accordance with a permission granted under this Act is contained in sub-section 2. Sub-section 3 provides that a person who contravenes this prohibition shall be guilty of an offence and shall be liable on summary conviction to a fine not exceeding £20 and for each day of a continuing offence after conviction of £10. In addition to being prosecuted under section 24, a person who contravenes this section may have an enforcement notice served on him under section 31 requiring him to restore the land to its original condition. If he fails so to restore the land the planning authority may itself after a period of not less than one month enter the land, restore it and recover as a simple contract debt from the owner of the land the reasonable costs of so doing.[1]

An enforcement notice may require the removal or alteration of any structures, the discontinuance of any use of land or the carrying out on land of any works.[2]

Applications for Permission

The processing of planning applications is governed by section 26 of the 1963 Act and by the regulations made under this Act and the 1976 Act.[3] The main steps to be taken by an applicant for planning permission are set out in Appendix 1(a) to this book. If an indication of what kind of development would be permitted is required, an application for outline permission only need be made. The steps to be taken in this case are easier and less expensive but such a permission is granted only 'subject to the subsequent approval of the planning authority',[4] and does not of itself authorise

41

the carrying out of any development until an approval has been applied for and obtained.[5]

An applicant for permission, outline permission or approval is required to publish notice of his application in a newspaper or on a notice on the land in question, all in the prescribed manner and to submit such plans and particulars as are required by the regulations. This newspaper notice should state the nature and extent of the development[6] and in the case of *Keleghan & Others* v. *Corby & Others*[7] a planning permission was declared invalid by McMahon J. because of a failure to give due notice:

> I am quite satisfied of one thing, that the advertisement published by the applicants . . . was entirely inadequate to put the public who might be concerned on notice of what the permission required involved. The purpose of the notice is to give members of the public who may be concerned with the development an idea whether the development looked for is the kind that may affect their interest . . . Accordingly for that reason in my view the grant of permission was not validly granted.[8]

The regulations provide for the public display at the offices of the planning authority of the plans, drawings, maps and particulars accompanying each planning application pending the determination thereof,[9] and also for the notification by the planning authority of certain specified bodies such as An Taisce or Bord Fáilte Éireann in certain circumstances.[10]

Once an application is made to a planning authority a decision one way or another must be made. The planning authority may decide to grant the permission, to grant it subject to conditions or to refuse it.[11] Even if the planning authority do nothing about the application a decision to grant the permission or approval is deemed to have been given after the expiry of a specified period,[12] such period to commence in cases where further information, evidence or publication is required, when the applicant complies with such requirement.[13] This period can now be extended with the consent of the applicant.[14]

Where the decision is to grant permission the authority does not actually make the grant until the time for taking an appeal has passed or if an appeal has been taken until it has been withdrawn. If the Board decides to grant permission or approval it makes the grant as soon as maybe after so deciding.[15]

In dealing with an application for planning permission or approval the authority 'shall be restricted to considering the proper planning and development of the area of the authority (including the preservation and improvement of the amenities thereof), regard being had to the provisions of the development plan, [and] the provisions of any special amenity area order relating to the said area . . .'

If a planning authority decides to grant planning permission subject to conditions, there are several groups of conditions listed in the 1963 Act which it may impose. Some of the more important of these are: conditions regulating the development of adjoining land; conditions requiring the carrying out of works (such as car-parks) necessary for the purpose of the development; conditions requiring provision of open spaces; or of landscaping; conditions requiring the construction of roads, sewers and water mains in excess of the immediate needs of the proposed development (subject to the payment of a contribution by the local authority);[16] and conditions requiring the removal of any structures authorised by the permission at the end of any specified period.

Where a planning authority either refuses to grant a permission or approval or gives the grant subject to conditions it must state the reasons for its refusal or the imposition of conditions in the decision and in the notification of it to the applicant.[17]

A person is not entitled to carry out development solely by reason of a permission or approval granted under the Planning Acts.[18]

One does not need to have a legal estate or interest in the property which is the subject of one's planning application, let alone be the owner thereof. This does not mean, however, that any person can apply for planning permission as was made clear by Henchy J. in his judgment in *Frescati Estates Ltd.* v. *Marie Walker:*[19]

> For my part I have no difficulty in accepting that the choice of the word *applicant* and the deliberate avoidance of the use of any word or expression to suggest that the person seeking permission should have any legal estate or interest in the property show that the legislature did not intend that possession of such estate or interest by the person applying was to be necessary . . .

Appeals

Provision is made for an appeal against any decision of a planning authority by section 26 (5) of the 1963 Act and the procedure to be followed is laid down in this sub-section and also in the regulations dealing with appeals and references.[20] The applicant for planning permission is entitled to appeal[21] against the refusal of a planning authority to grant permission but he cannot confine his appeal to the imposition of conditions upon such grant: the appeal will be dealt with as if it were a *de novo* application[22] and accordingly an appellant concerned with having an onerous condition removed can end up with an outright refusal. He is entitled to make his appeal (which should be in writing and should state the subject matter of the appeal, the grounds of the appeal and should be accompanied by a deposit of £10[23]) within one month beginning on the day of receipt by him of the decision of the planning authority[24] and any other party is entitled to appeal within twenty-one days beginning on the day of the giving of the decision.[25]

In determining an appeal the Board must deal with it as if it were an application in the first instance, and the provisions of the 1963 Act applicable to first instance applications to planning authorities shall apply to its determination of an appeal. If the Board wishes to have regard to any considerations relating to the proper planning and development of the area which were not put before it by the parties to the appeal and which were not brought to its notice, then it must afford them an opportunity to make observations on these considerations.[26] The regulations provide generally that each party to an appeal must be given the documents lodged by the other parties and an opportunity to comment thereon.[27]

Any party[28] to an appeal or reference may request an oral hearing. By section 16 of the 1976 Act the Board has absolute discretion whether or not to hold an oral hearing on any reference or appeal subject only to a power to direct such a hearing vested in the Minister.

The conduct of such oral hearings is regulated by section 26 (5) and section 82 (as amended) of the 1963 Act and by articles 35 to 48 of the 1977 regulations. The general effect of these provisions is now very briefly described.

As already indicated, the Board is obliged to deal with the appeal as if it were an application in the first instance. In cases where an oral hearing is requested, the Board will usually appoint a person[29] invariably referred to as an 'inspector' to take charge of such hearings and this person is given power to take evidence on oath and to administer oaths, and sworn witnesses are given the same immunities and privileges as if they were witnesses in the High Court. The inspector may summon an officer of a planning authority to give evidence and such officer must comply with such an order; an inspector may visit and inspect any land to which the reference or appeal relates and he may require the attendance of any person to give evidence or to produce any documents subject to the provision that the reasonable and necessary expenses incurred by such a witness if he has had to travel more than ten miles from his ordinary place of residence, shall be paid by the planning authority at the request of the inspector.[30] A request for an oral hearing must be made in writing and usually takes the form of a letter addressed to An Bord Pleanála.

It is important to note that in order to comply strictly with article 36 (c) of the regulations, such a letter should state the grounds of appeal. The practice did exist of merely stating in such letters that the grounds of appeal will be submitted at a later date. Such a letter would not be in strict conformity with the regulations. The correct course is to include in such a letter all grounds of appeal which may be very shortly stated and expanded later if this is thought desirable.[31] Further, since by section 26 of the 1963 Act an appeal is dealt with as if it were a first instance application the Board is not restricted to a consideration only of the matters referred to as grounds of appeal and section 17 of the 1976 Act specifically provides for cases when the Board takes into account considerations other than those put before it by the parties to the appeal.

The Board has discretion as to the conduct of the hearing and, in particular, is required to conduct the hearing without due formality, decide the order of appearance of the parties, permit any party to appear in person or to be represented by another person and to hear, if it thinks fit, any person who is not a party to the appeal or reference.[32]

Finally, in the case of an oral hearing conducted by an inspector, he is required to furnish a report thereon to the Board or the Minister as the case may be and this report must be considered before a decision is made. Note especially that the inspector is obliged to include a recommendation in this report.[33]

As has already been pointed out the role of the inspector in the conduct of such an oral hearing and in the preparation of his report to the Minister had been dealt with in many Irish cases, the general effect of which was to reduce his role to that of president over the proceedings at the oral hearing. He has power to take evidence on oath and to hear parties at his discretion, subject to the regulations already referred to, and once the oral hearing is complete his role as defined in recent judgments of the Irish superior courts became little more than that of a reporter who was required only to furnish a fair and accurate account of these proceedings but who had no duty to advise the Minister as to the importance of any evidence or as to how the issue should be determined.[34] Indeed, under these decisions made prior to the coming into force of section 23 of the 1976 Act, if the inspector included such advice or included material in his report not ventilated at the oral hearing and if it could not be shown that the Minister specifically ignored such advice or material in arriving at his decision, then it was open to review.

This reduction in the role of the inspector was regarded as unsatisfactory in that qualified engineers or other expert persons were appointed to take charge of oral hearings in both planning and compulsory acquisition cases and the purpose behind this practice was to ensure that such inspectors would appreciate any technical evidence produced and would be in a position to offer the Minister advice in relation to his decision should he want it. These or similar considerations appear to have prompted the inclusion of the requirement in section 23 of the 1976 Act that an inspector's report shall include a recommendation thus restoring to him a significant role in relation to the making of decisions.

Finally, if a question of law arises on any appeal, the question may be referred to the High Court by the appeal tribunal and any party may appeal to the same court within three months after the giving of the decision or such longer period as the High Court may allow.[35]

Constitution, Jurisdiction and Procedure of the Planning Board
This Board is established[36] by section 3 of the 1976 Act and consists of a chairman who is to be an acting or former High Court judge together with four ordinary members. The Board determines matters by a majority of votes of members present. Section 6 of

the 1976 Act empowers the Minister to give general policy directives to the Board but not to interfere in any particular appeal. Section 16 of the 1976 Act gives the Board absolute discretion whether or not to hold an oral hearing and section 20 provides for new regulations to be made by the Minister for oral hearings. Note that under section 23 reports on oral hearings must include a recommendation which is to be considered by the Minister or the Board before the issue is determined. Section 14 (8) is an important sub-section which enables the Board to grant a planning permission or approval even if the proposed development materially contravenes the relevant development plan or a special amenity area order.

The following is a list of the more important appeals and references transferred to the Board by the 1976 Act:

(a)   against a decision of a planning authority under section 26 of the 1963 Act on an application for permission or approval to carry out development

(b)   against a decision for permission for retention under section 27

(c)   against revocation or modification of permission under section 30

(d)   against an enforcement notice under section 33

(e)   against a notice requiring removal or alteration of any structure under section 36

(f)   against a notice requiring discontinuance of use under section 37

(g)   against notices involving a hedge (section 44), a tree (section 45) or conservation (section 46)

(h)   against an order creating a public right-of-way over land (section 48)

(i)   relating to cables, wires or pipelines (section 85)

(j)   relating to licences (section 89).

The Board has also jurisdiction in relation to appeals arising out of the new 'withering' provisions of section 29 of the 1976 Act.

Compensation

If a planning permission has been refused or has been granted subject to conditions, the applicant may be entitled either to require the planning authority to purchase the lands in question in certain cases or to be paid compensation for a consequent reduction in their value.

If on appeal, planning permission has been refused or granted subject to conditions and the applicant claims:

(a)   that the land has become incapable of reasonably beneficial use in its existing state, and

(b)   that it cannot be rendered capable of reasonably beneficial use by carrying out any permitted development, and

(c)   where permission has been granted subject to conditions, that the land cannot be rendered capable of reasonably beneficial use by developing it in accordance with those conditions,

he may within three months of the decision require the planning authority to purchase his interest in the land.[37] If the planning authority agrees to purchase the land, a notice is served on the applicant to that effect which has the same effect as if it were a compulsory purchase order.

If the planning authority is not willing to purchase the land the matter comes before the Minister[38] who may confirm the purchase notice (which then becomes effective as a compulsory purchase order), refuse to confirm it, revoke any conditions attached to the granting of the permission or amend them or direct that some other permission be given in respect of the land, if it appears to him that the land or part of it could be rendered capable of reasonably beneficial use.

A far more common form of application is by a person who claims that his or her interest in the land has been reduced by reason of the refusal of permission to develop land or the grant of permission subject to conditions. Under this form of relief, provided by section 55 of the 1963 Act, the owner of an interest in the land can be compensated to the extent of any reduction of the value of his interest and an occupier can be compensated in respect of damage to his trade, business or profession carried on on the land. A claim for compensation under section 55 must be made within six months of the decision of the planning authority or the Board or longer at the discretion of the Circuit Court. If a planning authority is required to purchase an interest in land pursuant to section 29 of the 1963 Act, no compensation in respect of that interest can be paid under section 55. Again, when calculating the amount of compensation, regard must be had to any permission under the Act to develop the land, either existing or promised, and any exempted development which may be carried out on the land. Moreover, the reduction in value is to be calculated on the basis that if the permission had been granted certain conditions relating to minimum building standards, a contribution by the developer towards expenditure on works facilitating the proposed development and relating to the giving of security by the developer for completion of the development would have been imposed. Further, it is to be assumed that apart from these and other exempted items, no permission for any development would have been granted in respect of the land under the 1963 Act.

The 1963 Act, however, sets out in section 56 a long list of cases where compensation will not apply. These cases are broken down into instances where permission is refused and instances where permission is granted subject to conditions.

Examples of cases where compensation will not be payable for a refusal to grant planning permission include cases where the development consists of or includes the making of any material change in use;[39] or where the development would be premature by reference to a deficiency in water supplies or sewerage facilities or because a road lay-out for the area has not been indicated in the development plan; or where the development would endanger public safety by reason of traffic hazard or obstruction of road-users; or where one of the reasons for the refusal is the necessity to preserve any view or prospect of special amenity value or special interest; or where the development is in an area to which a special amenity area order relates; or where a reason for the refusal is that a development comprising any structure or addition or extension of a structure would infringe an existing building line, would be under a public road, would seriously injure the amenities or depreciate the value of property in the vicinity, would tend to create serious traffic congestion, would endanger the health or safety of persons occupying or employed in the structure or any adjoining structure or would be prejudicial to public health.

Further, compensation will not be payable if the development would contravene materially a condition attached to an existing development permission.

There is also a long list of conditions which prelude the operation of the compensation provisions. This list is to be found in section 56 of the 1963 Act and in the Third Schedule (parts 2, 3 and 4) and is too long to be set out extensively here. These conditions relate to good building and design standards, conditions relating to zoning, congestion, planning and services, and amenities generally including conditions relating to preserving land for public parks, dumps, rights-of-way and conditions relating to the preservation of items of archaeological and historical interest, preserving ruins and preserving woods, trees, shrubs, plants and flowers. In addition, no condition relating to a matter in respect of which a requirement could have been imposed under any other Act or statutory instrument without liability for compensation can attract compensation. Finally, by section 41 (c) of the 1976 Act conditions designed to reduce vibrations or noise which could become a nuisance to neighbours are included in this class. Such conditions can be imposed by virtue of section 39 (c) of the 1976 Act.

Moreover, by section 57 of the 1963 Act even if compensation would otherwise be payable in a case where planning permission is refused compensation is not payable if there is available for the land permission for development of a residential, commercial or industrial character.

By section 58 the Minister has discretion to order payment of compensation which could not otherwise be payable if application had been made to him within (but not after) two months after notification of the adverse decision and he is satisfied that it would. not be just and reasonable in the particular circumstances to withhold compensation. This jurisdiction has been extended by section 41 (e) of the 1976 Act to cases involving the revocation or modification of permission. All compensation payable under the Planning Acts can be recovered from the relevant authority as a simple contract debt in any court of competent jurisdiction.[40]

The planning authority must keep a register of all compensation payments in excess of £20[41] and these may be recovered if the payee develops the relevant lands within fourteen years.[42]

Appendix One

(A) Procedure for applying for planning permission

General

Planning permission must be granted prior to the commencement of any development which is not exempt.

'Development' in the planning sense means the carrying out of any work on, in or under land or the making of any material change in the use of any structure or other land. Material change includes the conversion of a single dwelling-house into flats.

As the onus is on the developer to obtain permission it is advisable for him to consult with the planning authority before commencing work.

Application may be made for:

(a) outline permission which is subject to the subsequent approval of the planning authority

(b) permission.

An outline application can be made where some indication of the planning authority's attitude to the proposed development is required before having detailed plans prepared.

Application Procedure

No official application form is necessary but the following must be supplied:

(a) name and address of applicant

(b) particulars of applicant's interest in the property

(c) a copy of a newspaper circulating in the area in which the land or structure is situate (and preferably published during the two weeks immediately prior to the application) and in which there has been published a notice with the following particulars:

    (i) as a heading, the names of the area and the city, town or county

    (ii) name of applicant

    (iii) location of land or the address of the structure

    (iv) extent and nature of the development for which permission or approval is sought

    (v) in cases where retention permission is sought, nature of proposed use and period of proposed retention

    (vi) nature of continued use, where application relates to continuance of any use;

Alternatively, a notice may be erected or fixed on the land or structure setting out the following:

     (i)   notice must be headed 'Application to Planning Authority'
     (ii) name of applicant to be given
     (iii) nature and extent of the proposed development to be stated
     (iv) notice must be erected on or near the main entrance from the public road or any other part of the land adjoining the public road and must be capable of being read by road users or if not, its location must be indicated on a plan accompanying the planning application
     (v)   a copy of the above notice must accompany the application
(d) plans, drawings and maps etc. as follows:
     (i)   plans (including a site or layout plan and drawings of floor plans, elevations and sections) and other particulars necessary to identify the land and to describe the works or structure;
and where the application consists of or mainly consists of application for change or continuance of use:
     (ii) (a) a statement with particulars giving the nature and extent of existing and proposed uses
           (b) a plan or location map on which the land effected is identified
           (c) plans similar to those at (i) above in relation to any works.

Outline Permission

Applications for outline permission need be accompanied only by such plans and particulars as are necessary to identify the land and enable the authority to determine the siting, layout or other proposals but a consequent application for approval must comply with the requirements for applications for full permission.

Plans, drawings and maps

These must be in duplicate and comply with the following requirements:
(a) buildings, roads, boundaries and other features in the vicinity must be shown on site plans and layout plans
(b) elevations should show main features of adjacent buildings
(c) elevations and sections must be drawn to scale, which must be indicated and the principal dimensions (including overall height) must appear in figures together with distances of the structures from boundaries
(d) the north point should appear on maps and plans
(e) reconstruction, alteration or extension works should be distinguished by colour or otherwise from existing structures
(f) the name and address of the person who prepares the plans must appear.

Further Information

A planning authority may require the publication of a further notice or the production of further particulars or plans, etc. (including not more than two additional copies of plans, etc.) or further information generally or reasonable evidence in support of the information given.

(B) Procedure for appealing a planning decision

General

Before the expiration of two months (or such extended period as may be agreed by the applicant) following the submission of a valid planning application (or from the day on which the applicant complies with a notice requiring the production of further information or evidence) a notification should be issued to the applicant indicating the planning authority's decision. Notification of intention to grant does not entitle the applicant to commence work as this requires the grant of permission. The reason for the delay in issuing a grant is to allow a third party to appeal and if this is successful no grant is issued.

Appeals

An applicant may appeal against a planning authority's decision within one month commencing on the day of the receipt by him of the decision and a third party may appeal within 21 days beginning on the day of the giving of the decision. There is no special form of appeal but the same should be in writing, addressed to An Bord Pleanála, Holbrook House, Holles Street, Dublin 2 (Tel. 763901). It should set out the grounds of the appeal, and be accompanied by a deposit of £10.

(C) Procedure for applying to court for an injunction
(see rules of the Superior Courts (No. 1) 1976).

This application is brought under section 27 of the 1976 Act by way of motion on notice to the person against whom relief is sought.

This notice is entitled 'In the matter of the Local Government (Planning and Development) Act 1976 and should set out the relief sought; describe the land or development affected; the name and place for service of the person seeking relief; the date (except in urgent cases at least ten days after service) upon which it is proposed to apply to court; and this notice must be filed in the Central Office of the High Court.

Notice of the motion is given to the person against whom relief is sought and the court has power to direct service on any person who should be notified or to dismiss the application for want of such service.

There must be at least ten days between service of the notice and the day named for the hearing of the motion.

Evidence in support of the application should be by affidavit, filed in the Central Office and served with the notice. Any affidavit used in opposition shall also be filed in the Central Office and served on the applicant within seven days of the service on the respondent of the applicant's affidavit.

If satisfied that delay might entail irreparable or serious mischief, the court may make an order in the nature of an injunction *ex parte* (i.e. in the absence of the respondent). There are no special requirements for the contents of the affidavit supporting the application but it should contain in so far as possible a statement of the interest of the respondent(s) in the land, a history of the use of the land or structures

Note: 35. S. 82 (3) and (3A) as substituted by S. 42 of the 1976 Act. ·
tioning the validity of a decision of a planning authority or of the Board
or the Minister must be instituted within two months of the decision[35].

and details of any unauthorised development supported by the best evidence available, an indication that the unauthorised use or development is continuing or imminent or whatever the case may be, and the position as regards planning permission if this is known, together with some indication of the character (zoning, etc.) of the area in which the subject land is situate.

Appendix Two

Statutory rules for the assessment of compensation

(Note: Rules 1 - 6 inclusive are contained in section 2 of the Acquisition of Land (Assessment of Compensation) Act 1919; Rules 7 - 16 inclusive are contained in the Fourth Schedule to the Local Government (Planning and Development) Act 1963 and are inserted into section 2 of the 1919 Act by section 69 of the 1963 Act).

(1)   No allowance shall be made on account of the acquisition being compulsory.

(2)   The value of land shall, subject as hereinafter provided, be taken to be the amount which the land if sold in the open market by a willing seller might be expected to realise: provided always that the arbitrator shall be entitled to consider all returns and assessments of capital value for taxation made or acquiesced in by the claimant.

(3)   The special suitability or adaptability of the land for any purpose shall not be taken into account if that purpose is a purpose to which it could be applied only in pursuance of statutory powers, or for which there is no market apart from the special needs of a particular purchaser or the requirements of any government department or any local or public authority: provided that any bona fide offer for the purchase of the land made before the passing of this Act which may be brought to the notice of the arbitrator shall be taken into consideration.

(4)   Where the value of the land is increased by reason of the use thereof or of any premises thereon in a manner which could be restrained by any court, or is contrary to law, or is detrimental to the health of the inmates of the premises or to the public health, the amount of the increase shall not be taken into account.

(5)   Where land is, and but for the compulsory acquisition would continue to be, devoted to a purpose of such a nature that there is no general demand or market for land for that purpose, the compensation may, if the official arbitrator is satisfied that reinstatement in some other place is bona fide intended, be assessed on the basis of the reasonable cost of equivalent reinstatement.

(6)   The provisions of rule 2 shall not affect the assessment of compensation for disturbance or any other matter not directly based on the value of land.

(7)   In the case of a compulsory acquisition of buildings, the reference in rule 5 to the reasonable cost of equivalent reinstatement shall be taken as a reference to that cost not exceeding the estimated cost of buildings such as would be capable of serving an equivalent purpose

55

over the same period of time as the buildings compulsorily acquired
would have done, having regard to any structural depreciation in those
buildings.

(8) The value of the land shall be calculated with due regard to any restrictive covenant entered into by the acquirer when the land is compulsorily acquired.

(9) Regard shall be had to any restriction on the development of the land in respect of which compensation has been paid under the Local Government (Planning and Development) Act 1963.

(10) Regard shall be had to any restriction on the development of the land which could, without conferring a right to compensation, be imposed under any Act or under any order, regulation, rule or bye-law made under any Act.

(11) Regard shall not be had to any depreciation or increase in value attributable to:
(a) the land, or any land in the vicinity thereof, being reserved for any particular purpose in a development plan, or
(b) inclusion of the land in a special amenity area order.

(12) No account shall be taken of any value attributable to any unauthorised structure or unauthorised use.

(13) No account shall be taken of:
(a) the existence of proposals for development of the land or any other land by a local authority, or
(b) the possibility or probability of the land or other land becoming subject to a scheme of development undertaken by a local authority.

(14) Regard shall be had to any contribution which a planning authority would have required as a condition precedent to the development of the land.

(15) In rules 9, 10, 11, 12, 13 and 14 'development', 'development plan', 'special amenity area order', 'unauthorised structure', 'unauthorised use', 'local authority' and 'the appointed day' have the same meanings respectively as in the Local Government (Planning and Development) Act 1963.

(16) In the case of land incapable of reasonably beneficial use which is purchased by a planning authority under section 29 of the Local Government (Planning and Development) Act 1963, the compensation shall be the value of the land exclusive of any allowance for disturbance or severance.

Notes to Chapter One

1. This merger in practice of the rights of an individual who joins a trade union is not, of course, recognised by law. The Constitution in article 40.6.1.iii vests the right of association in individual citizens, not in trade unions, and accordingly, for example, the question of whether or not a trade dispute exists between a picketing workman and his employer will not be affected by whether or not the strike is officially recognised by his union.

2. See J. A. G. Griffith and H. Street, *Principles of Administrative Law,* (London: Pitman & Sons Ltd., 4th ed., 1967) Chapter I

3. *Cooper* v. *Wandsworth Board of Works,* (1863 14 CB (NS)180). For an account of this case see H.W.R. Wade, *Administrative Law* (Clarendon Press, Oxford; Third Edition, 1971) at pp. 189-190 and Heuston, *Essays in Constitutional Law* (Stevens & Sons 1964) at pp. 185 ff.

4. Hear the other side.

5. In England, at least, there is the Tribunals and Inquiries Act, 1958, which adopted several recommendations made by the report of the Committee on Administrative Tribunals and Inquiries (The Franks Report), Cmnd 218 of 1957.

6. Constitution, article 34.3.2.

7. See Loren P. Beth, *The Development of Judicial Review in Ireland, 1937-1966* (Dublin: Institute of Public Administration, 1967), p. 64.

8. The Trade Disputes Act 1906, for example, can be seen as the outcome of a sustained contest between Parliament and the judges in England.

9. See Beth, op. cit., Table 2, which contains a summary of decisions of unconstitutionality.

10. Article 6.

11. Article 37.

12. For example where Kenny J. in *Central Dublin Development Association Ltd. and Others* v. *Attorney General* (109 I L T R 69) relied on the doctrine of the separation of powers under article 6 to avoid an earlier decision which could have reduced his jurisdiction over administrative bodies. And see *The Irish Jurist* VI (New Series) Part 1, for an article by J. M. Kelly, 'Judicial Review of Administrative Action: New Irish Trends'. pp. 43-44.

13. Article 34.5.1 contains the oath sworn by judges to the effect *inter alia* that they will uphold the Constitution. See also J. M. Kelly, *Fundamental Rights in the Irish Law and Constitution* (Dublin: Allen Figgis; Second ed.) p. 260, on the question of the removal of judges under the Constitution.

14. Donal Barrington, SC, writing in *The Irish Jurist* VIII (New Series) Part 1, 'Private Property under the Irish Constitution', pp. 1-17 at p. 12 where he is commenting on this case (1972 I R 241). Compare the celebrated words of Byles J. in *Cooper* v. *Wandsworth Board of Works* (1863) 14 C B (NS)180: 'The justice of the common law will supply the ommission of the legislature,' *Byrne* v. *Ireland* reported at 1972 I R 241.

15. 1965 I R 294. See Kelly, op. cit., pp. 121-123.

16. *Educational Company of Ireland* v. *FitzPatrick & Others* (1961 I R 345; 96 I L T and S J 147).

17. See Kelly, op. cit., pp. 41-48 for a discussion of the advantages and disadvantages of this kind of assertive review by Irish judges of the Acts of the Oireachtas.

18. 109 I L T R 69 at p. 86. See generally Donal Barrington, loc. cit., for a discussion of property rights under the Irish Constitution.

19. 1974 I R 284.

20. See p. 313.

21. 1972 I R 241.

22. 1950 I R 67.

23. See p. 310.

24. See for example Wade, op. cit., pp. 171-218, for a general discussion of the application of natural justice principles to the administration and Kelly, op. cit., (pp. 305-308) for a short treatment of this topic in the Irish context. Note that Kelly distinguishes a third rule of natural justice which he calls 'non-retroactivity of criminal sanctions'.
    In some recent Irish decisions the phrase 'constitutional justice' has been used by judges and seems to include more than natural justice. The phrase is nowhere defined but in *McDonald* v. *Bord na gCon* (1965 I R 217 at p. 242) Walsh J. noted: 'In the context of the Constitution, natural justice might be more appropriately termed constitutional justice and must be understood to import more than the two well-established principles that no man shall be judge of his own cause and *audi alteram partem.'* The same judge in *East Donegal Co-Operative Livestock Mart Ltd. and Others* v. *Attorney General* (1970 I R 317 at p. 341) observed as follows: '. . . the presumption of constitutionality carries with it not only the presumption that the constitutional interpretation or construction is the one intended by the Oireachtas but also that the Oireachtas intended that proceedings, procedures, discretions and adjudications which are permitted, provided for or prescribed by an Act of the Oireachtas are to be conducted in accordance with the principles of constitutional justice.' At p. 338 the same judge includes a passage which suggests that there is a constitutionally guaranteed right of procedure whereby a citizen who apprehends an invasion of a constitutional right by the operation of a statute or possibly even by an act or decision of a local authority, whether that right be his own or that of another, may challenge the relevant authority on this ground in the Irish courts. It seems then that the principles of constitutional justice lay down more rigorous standards of fair procedure than those of natural justice. (See a note by James O'Reilly in *The Irish Jurist*

VIII (New Series) at p. 299 where *Glover* v. *BLN* (1973 I R 388) is under discussion).

This concept of constitutional justice as something over and above natural justice has only recently emerged. It has been referred to at some length by O'Higgins C. J. in *The State (Healy)* v. *Donoghue* (1976 I R 325) in the following terms: 'Where a man's liberty is at stake or where he faces a very severe penalty which may affect his welfare or his livelihood justice may require more than the application of normal and fair procedures to his trial. Facing as he does the power of the State which is his accuser, he may be unable adequately to defend himself because of ignorance, lack of education, youth or other incapacity. In such circumstances his plight may require, if justice is to be done, that he should have legal assistance. In such circumstances if he cannot provide such assistance by reason of lack of means, does justice under the Constitution also require that he be aided in his defence? In my view it does.

'The general view of what is fair and proper in relation to criminal trials has always been the subject of change and development. Rules of evidence and rules of procedure gradually evolved as notions of fairness developed. The right to speak and to give evidence and the right to be represented by a lawyer of one's choice were gradually recognised. Today many people would be horrified to learn how far it was necessary to travel to right the balance between the accuser and the accused. If the right to be represented is now an acknowledged right of an accused person, justice requires something more when because of lack of means a person facing a serious criminal charge cannot provide a lawyer for his own defence. In my view the concept of justice under the Constitution or constitutional justice to use the phrase used in the judgment of this court in *McDonald* v. *Bord na gCon* (1965 I R 217), *East Donegal Co-Operative Livestock Mart Ltd. and Others* v. *The Attorney General* (1970 I R 317) and the majority judgment of this court in *Glover* v. *BLN* (1973 I R 388), requires that in such circumstances the person charged must be afforded the opportunity of being represented. This opportunity must be provided by the State. Only in this way can justice be done, and only by recognising and discharging this duty can the State be said to vindicate the personal rights of the person charged.' Constitutional justice might be said to be the principles of fair procedures required by the Constitution and these would seem to include a right to legal aid in certain cases. See also, J. P. Casey in *The Irish Jurist* VII (New Series) Part 1 at p. 1: 'Reform of collective bargaining law: some constitutional implications' for a comment on this subject.

25. See Kelly, op. cit., pp. 311-324, for a discussion of the application of these principles of review by Irish judges.

26. See Kelly in *The Irish Jurist* VI (New Series) Part 1, p. 40 ff. 'Judicial Review of Administration: New Irish Trends'.

27. 1972 I R 241.

28. For a comprehensive analysis of this case see Osborough in *The Irish*

Jurist VII (New Series) p. 275 ff. 'The demise of the State's immunity in tort'. See also Kelly, *op. cit.*, pp. 324-349.

Notes to Chapter Two

1. For *Murphy No. 1* see 1972 I R 215. For *Murphy No. 2* see 1976 I R 143. For *Murphy No. 3* see unreported judgments of Butler J. (High Court) and Henchy J. (Supreme Court) delivered respectively on 31 July 1975 and 21 November 1975. For the sake of completeness it can be noted that a further case was brought by this plaintiff claiming interest on unpaid compensation at equitable rates and not at 5% as contended for by Dublin Corporation. In this last case the Supreme Court (unreported judgment delivered 29 July 1977) reversing McMahon J. (who in a judgment dated 21 February 1977 and delivered in the High Court had upheld the Corporations's contention) held the plaintiff entitled to interest at the rate 'at which, on the date of entry (on the land) the local authority could borrow from the local loans fund' which in practice means considerably more than 5%. This decision reversed that of Dixon J. in *Norton* v. *Dublin Corporation* (1959 *Irish Jurist* Reports p. 62).
2. A notice to treat fixes the date in relation to which the value of lands taken is to be compensated.
3. In *In re Deansrath Investment Co. Ltd.* (1974 I R 228).
4. Unreported judgment delivered 21 November 1975. The other members of the court were O'Higgins C. J. and Griffin J. both of whom agreed this judgment. This judgment reversed on both questions the High Court judgment of Butler J. delivered 31 July 1975. For a fuller discussion of this case see Ch. 4 below.
5. On the grounds that the first notice to treat was served after the 'determination' of the proceedings despite the subsequent appeal from such final determination.
6. The *Murphy No. 1* decision was applied to criminal cases by O'Higgins C. J. in *Ferguson's* case in a judgment delivered 28 October 1975 (unreported: see *The Irish Times*, 29 October 1975).
7. See *Duncan* v. *Cammel Laird & Co. Ltd.* 1942 A C 624.
8. 1959 I R 105.
9. 1968 A C 910.
10. 1972 I R at p. 237.
11. 1956 S C 1.
12. 1972 I R at p. 237.
13. See pp. 237-239.
14. See p. 238.
15. Unreported: judgment delivered 1 March 1974.

16. See p. 19 of the judgment.
17. See pp. 23-24.
18. Under the Planning Act 1976 the decision becomes that of the Planing Board. The changes in the law effected by the Planning Act 1976 are discussed more fully in Chs. 4 and 5 hereafter but it is worth noting that the new Act gives the Board discretion whether or not to hold an oral hearing (section 17) and power to conduct the same through or by any person duly appointed by it (Schedule 1, article 24).
19. The portion of the judgment referred to is that already quoted at p. 14.
20. This is a new provision. See also the decision of the Supreme Court in *Geraghty* v. *Minister for Local Government* (1976 I R 153).
21. 1976 I R 143, see p. 149.
22. See pp. 167-168.
23. See p. 174.
24. 1971 I R 217, p. 264.
25. See judgment of Lord Justice Atkin in *Rex* v. *The Electricity Commissioners* (1924 1 K B 171).
26. Case reported at 1976 I R 143 ff. High Court judgment delivered 14 December 1972, not reported.
27. See pp. 4-5.
28. Unreported: judgment delivered in the High Court 31 January 1973.
29. See p. 4.
30. See per Kenny J. in *Kiely* v. *Minister for Social Welfare* (1971 I R 21 at p. 25) and J. M. Kelly in 'Judicial Review of Administrative Actions: New Irish Trends' in *The Irish Jurist* VI (New Series), Part 1, at pp. 46-47.
31. 1976 I R 153. See judgments of Walsh J. at p. 172 and Gannon J. at p. 184. Compare generally the judgment of Finlay P. in *Killiney and Ballybrack Development Association Limited* v. *The Minister for Local Government and Templefinn Estates Ltd.* (unreported; judgment delivered in the High Court 1 March 1974 at pp. 13-16).
32. 1970 I R 317.
33. 1965 I R 217, p. 242.
34. *Fuller* v. *Dublin County Council* (1976 I R 20).
35. *International Trading Ltd.* v. *Corporation of Dublin* (1974 I R 373).

Notes to Chapter Three

1. 1970 I R 317.
2. 1976 I R 143.
3. See p. 146.
4. See p. 148.
5. 1954 I R 233.
6. See p. 149.

7. Judgment of the High Court delivered by Kenny J. on 7 October 1974 (reported 109 I L T R 57) and of the Supreme Court delivered by Henchy J. on 13 November 1975 (unreported).

8. Note, however, that a distinction is made in both judgments between compulsory acquisition made under section 76 of the Housing Act 1966 (immediate requirement) and section 77 (long-term needs). It might be an essential requirement in the former case to show 'at least a reasonable expectation that permission will be forthcoming' (Henchy J. at p. 6 of the judgment) whereas the extended section 77 power 'of its nature excludes the necessity of giving proof of having obtained permission'.

9. See p. 58. Compare *Hendron* v. *Dublin Corporation* (1943 I R 566) where Gavan-Duffy J. held that where land was proposed to be acquired by a local authority under the Housing Acts for the purposes of Part 3 of the Housing of the Working Classes Act 1890, section 38 of the Housing (Miscellaneous Provisions) Act 1931 conferred authority to take such land only on condition that it be taken by agreement and that no compulsory order could be made under section 37 unless the land comprised in the order was required immediately for housing purposes.

10. See pp. 60-61.

11. See p. 61.

12. 1976 I R 195.

13. See p. 189.

14. See p. 188.

15. See p. 189.

16. Which is mandatory; see p. 187.

17. See Appendix 2 for these rules as extended by the addition of rules 7 to 16 which are contained in the Fourth Schedule to the Local Government (Planning and Development) Act 1963.

18. 1974 I R 228.

19. 1909 1 K B at p. 29.

20. 1914 A C 569.

21. 1947 A C 565.

22. This dictum has been cited with approval by Lord Justice Parker in the case of *Lambe* v. *Secretary of State for War* (1955 2 Q B 612 at p. 662) and also by Lord Denning in the case of *Camrose (Viscount)* v. *Basingstoke Corporation* (1966 1 W L R 1100 at p. 1107) and both these endorsements were cited with approval by both Pringle J. and Budd J. in their respective judgments in the *Deansrath* case.

23. See p. 245.

24. Per Lord Justice Fletcher Moulton in the *Lucas and Chesterfield Gas and Waterboard* case.

25. 1974 I R at p. 245.

26. The *Deansrath* judgments were referred to with approval by Butler J. in *Murphy No. 3* who observed: 'Because of the detailed and authoritative nature of the judgments I can state principles without further elaboration'. (Unreported: judgment of Butler J. delivered in the High Court on 31 July 1975 and of the Supreme Court by Henchy J. on 21 November 1975).

27. See Chapter 1 at p. 10.
28. See pp. 2 and 3.
29. 'Determined', that is, pursuant to section 78 (3) (a) (ii) of the Housing
     Act 1966.
30. See p. 5.
31. See pp. 5-6.
32. See pp. 7-8. For *Murphy No. 1* see pp. 9, 11-15 and 60 (footnote 1).
33. See p. 10.
34. See Appendix 2.
35. See pp. 11-12.

Notes to Chapter Four

1. See per Butler J. in *Finn* v. *Bray UDC* (1974 I R 169 at p. 174): 'Of
    central importance in the new code is part three of the Act which
    imposes a statutory obligation on each planning authority to make a
    plan indicating the development objectives for its area', and see this
    case generally for the correct performance of obligations under the
    1963 Act, but compare section 37 of the 1976 Act and footnote 3
    below.
2. The Planning Board was established under section 3 of the 1976 Act on
    1 January 1977 by virtue of S. I. no. 308 of 1976. By virtue of S. I. no.
    56 of 1977 the Board was given responsibility for most planning appeals
    from 15 March 1977. Note that by section 39 (a) of the 1976 Act a
    planning authority is empowered to permit development which would
    materially contravene the development plan provided public notice is
    given and a manager must operate these provisions if a resolution is
    passed under section 4 of the City and County Management (Amend-
    ment) Act 1955.
3. See section 21 of the 1963 Act. This section has been significantly
    amended by section 37 of the 1976 Act to the general effect that an
    objecting ratepayer's right to be heard is reduced to a right to make
    written representations in cases involving amendment to proposed draft
    development plans or proposed draft variations.
4. See discussion below of *Frescati Estates Ltd.* v. *Marie Walker* (1975 I R
    177) and *Andrew B. Law* v. *Minister for Local Government and Trad-
    itional Homes Ltd.* (unreported: judgment of Deale J. delivered in the
    High Court 9 May 1974) for limitation of the category of person entitled
    to so participate.
5. In Part VI of the 1963 Act (sections 55-73).
6. Section 68 of the 1963 Act.
7. Section 74.
8. Section 76, as amended by section 43 (1) (i) of the 1976 Act.
9. By section 43 (k) of the 1976 Act (and compare also section 43 (d))

a planning authority may assist persons in providing homes for unwanted cats and dogs or may provide buildings for this purpose.

10. Section 77 (2).

11. Unreported: unauthorised judgment of McWilliam J. only available.

12. Unreported: judgment delivered by Kenny J. in the High Court on 30 March 1973.

13. My source of information is a person who was present on this occasion and who made a careful contemporary note.

14. Compare the following remarks of Johnston J. in *McCoy and Others* v. *Cork Corporation* (1934 I R 779 at p. 794): 'Then it is contended that the order should be quashed on the ground that it is bad *ex facie* . . . This is an argument that, with the limitation that I shall mention in a moment, I cannot accept. An order of a local authority under the Housing Acts, if it follows the prescribed form (as this one does), need not show jurisdiction on its face like the order of an inferior court. This was clearly decided in the case of *Kirkpatrick* v. *Borough of Maxwelltown* (1912 Sess. Cas. 288), in which it was held by the Court of Session that a closing order, which followed the statutory form, was not inept merely because it did not disclose the grounds of the order. In my opinion the contents of an order made by a local authority is only of importance in so far as it discloses or affords evidence of the fact that the authority had exceeded its powers or had failed to observe the requirements of the Legislature.'

15. See also sections 77 (4) (2) and 77 (1).

16. All regulations under the Planning Acts have now been consolidated as Local Government (Planning and Development) Regulations 1977 (S. I. no. 65 of 1977) which revokes all earlier regulations made under the Act of 1963.

17. By section 24 of the 1963 Act.

18. See section 2 of the 1963 Act – the interpretation section.

19. This arises because of the artificial meaning given to 'use' in section 2 of the 1963 Act. In *Viscount Securities Ltd.* (Unreported: judgment of Finlay P. delivered in the High Court 21 December 1976) which which concerned the construction of section 56 (1) (a) of the 1963 Act the two broad categories of development were defined as follows: 'One consists of works in the sense as defined of building, demolition, extension, alteration, repair or renewal and the second category being a change of user excluding such change as emanates from the act of building, demolition, extension, alteration or repair'. The sub-section of the Act under construction in that case appears at first sight to exclude from compensation virtually all development as virtually all development 'includes the making of any material change in the use of any structures or other land'. However, because of the artificial meaning given to 'use' and having regard to the definition of 'development' in section 3 of the 1963 Act this result was avoided. Compare Kenny J. in *The Central Dublin Development Association Limited and Others* v. *The Attorney General* (109 1 L T R 69).

20. By virtue of section 3 (2) and (3) of the 1963 Act.

21.   *Palser* v. *Grinling* (1948 A C 291).
22.   *Gilford RDC* v. *Fortiscue* (1959 2 Q B 112).
23.   1975 I R 177.
24.   Unreported: judgment delivered in the High Court 9 May 1974 by Deale J.
25.   This decision is surely consonant with the general objectives of the 1963 Act which provides for responsible public involvement in planning procedures. Indeed, as Henchy J. observed in the *Frescati* case concerning the interpretation of regulations made under the 1963 Act (quoting Lord Diplock in *Lawson* v. *Fox* 1974 1 A E R 783 at p. 786): 'It is legitimate to use the Act as an aid to the construction of the Regulations. To do the converse is to put the cart before the horse'.
26.   See Appendix 1 for the steps to be taken in making a planning application.
27.   S. I. no. 65 of 1977, Part 111 and Third Schedule.
28.   S. I. no. 65 of 1977, Third Schedule, Part 11 generally.
29.   In respect of camping sites so used prior to 1 October 1964 or in respect of which an enforcement notice has not been served within five years of the commencement of such use (see section (1) (a) of 1963 Act) the local authority may not be without a remedy whereby conditions attaching to the camp can be imposed for example, see section 34 of the Local Government (Sanitary Services) Act 1948.
30.   To the Planning Board by section 15 (2) of the 1976 Act.
31.   Section 5 (2).
32.   But see *The State (Modern Homes) (Ireland) Ltd.* v. *Dublin Corporation* (1953 I R 202) for a case in which it was held that once a planning authority had decided to make a scheme under the Town and Regional Planning Act 1934, they were obliged by virtue of section 29 of that Act to give effect to this decision and make such a scheme with all convenient speed. The plaintiffs in that case got an order directing the planning authority to make such a scheme within two years where the Corporation of Dublin had decided in 1934 to make such a scheme and had not done so by 1951.
33.   This list has been extended by section 43 (1) (e) of the 1976 Act.
34.   Section 21.
35.   The making of a development plan is made a reserved function by section 19 (17) of the 1963 Act. A reserved function is one which can be performed only by the elected members of the local authority as distinct from the manager.
36.   Section 20 (1); but by section 43 (f) of the 1976 Act the Minister may extend this period.
37.   Section 22 (3).
38.   Section 23.
39.   Section 31.
40.   Under sections 83 and 31 (5) of the 1963 Act.
41.   Section 73 (8).
42.   Under section 34 (1) of the 1963 Act.
43.   Section 34 (5) of the 1963 Act.

44. Section 27.
45. Sections 32 and 33 and see generally sections 31-37 for enforcement provisions.
46. See Appendix 1 (3) for procedure.

Notes to Chapter Five

1. Section 31 (5) of the 1963 Act, and see p. 38.
2. Section 31 (3) of the 1963 Act.
3. S.I. no. 65 of 1977 (Part IV).
4. Section 25 (2) (a).
5. See S.I. no. 65 of 1977; article 19 (5).
6. Article 15 (c).
7. Unreported; judgment of McMahon J. delivered in the High Court 12 November 1976.
8. Compare *dictum* in judgments delivered in the Supreme Court in *Ready-mix (Eire) Ltd.* v. *Dublin County Council and another* (unreported: Supreme Court judgments delivered 30 July 1974) and especially *dicta* of Griffin J. at p. 6: 'When any development of land is proposed, it is of fundamental importance that the proposal should be brought to the attention of the public and in particular to that of the residents of the neighbourhood in which the development is to take place'.
9. See S.I. no. 65 of 1977; article 29.
10. Article 25.
11. Section 26 (1). See *Dunne Ltd.* v. *Dublin County Council* (1974 I R 33 at pp. 54-55) for examples of 'conditions' which were held to be invalid by Pringle J. as either having 'no relation to the planning and development of the area' and being 'an unreasonable restriction which the defendants had no power to impose' or as being 'not sufficiently connected with the planning and development of the area, or the preservation or improvement of the amenities thereof.' The conditions were that the developers should notify all purchasers or tenants that the Department of Transport and Power had stated that aircraft noise would be significant in the area of the proposed development and, secondly, that modifications be carried out to the proposed houses in order 'to provide sound insulation in houses against aircraft noise.' These, the judge noted, were not made 'in the interests of the proper planning and development of the area', and both conditions were held invalid. By section 39 (c) of the 1976 Act a planning authority is authorised to include conditions relating to 'noise or vibration', and this is a non-compensatable condition (section 41 (c)).
12. Section 26 (4). For example (section 26 (4) (a) (iii)) on the expiry of two months beginning on the day of the receipt by the planning author-

ity of the application. See *The State (Murphy)* v. *Dublin County Council* (1970 I R 253) where it was decided that the posting of a Notice of Decision to refuse planning permission on a Friday was a sufficient notice to prevent the operation of section 26 (4) of the 1963 Act because the following Sunday was the last day of the relevant period within that section and despite the fact that the applicant did not in fact receive the notice until the following Monday because his office was not open for business on the intervening Saturday when the notice would have been delivered in the ordinary course of post. Compare *Dunne Ltd.* v. *Dublin County Council* (1974 I R 45) in which case the failure of the relevant planning authority to give notice of a decision relating to a planning application was held to have had the result that permission was deemed to have been given on the last day of the relevant period pursuant to section 26 (4).

13.   Section 26 (4) (b) (i).
14.   Section 26 (4A) inserted by section 39 (f) of the 1976 Act.
15.   Section 26 (9) (a) (b).
16.   Section 26 (7).
17.   Section 26 (8) as substituted by section 39 (g) of the 1976 Act.
18.   Section 26 (11) and see judgments of Kenny and Henchy JJ. in *Frescati Estates Ltd.* v. *Marie Walker* (1975 I R 177). Note also that provision is made (section 30) for the revocation or modification of a planning permission prior to commencement of works or change of use.
19.   1975 I R pp. 186, 190 and see p. 34 ante.
20.   S.I. no. 65 of 1977, Part V, articles 35-48.
21.   See Appendix One (b) p. 53 for steps to be taken.
22.   Section 26 (5) (b) of the 1963 Act and S.I. no. 65 of 1977; article 36.
23.   S.I. no. 65 of 1977; article 36.
24.   Section 26 (5) (c) (i).
25.   Section 25 (5) (c) (ii).
26.   Section 17 of the 1976 Act.
27.   Article 38.
28.   Article 35 (2) defines 'party' to an appeal as
    (a) the appellant
    (b) the planning authority against whose decision an appeal is made
    (c) the applicant for any permission, approval, licence or waiver notice in relation to which an appeal is made by another person (other than a person acting on behalf of the applicant)
    (d) any person served or issued by a planning authority with a notice or order, or copy thereof, under section 30, 33, 36, 37, 44, 45 or 48 of the Act of 1963 or section 25 of the Act of 1976, in relation to which an appeal is made by another person;
    and a 'party' to a reference as:
    (a) the person making the reference
    (b) the planning authority for the area in which the land or structure to which the particular reference relates is situated
    (c) any other person with whom the question to which the particular reference relates has arisen.

29. Invariably called an 'inspector' in practice. He is, however, referred to as a 'person' in section 82 of the 1963 Act.
30. Section 82 (4), (7).
31. See a lecture delivered on 20 March 1970 to the Society of Young Solicitors by E. M. Walsh, SC, entitled 'Local Government (Planning and Development) Act 1963: Planning Appeals', particularly at p. 2.
32. S. I. no. 65 of 1977 article 45. It should be remembered that apart from the discretion given to the inspector to hear any person who is not a party to the appeal or reference by article 45 (c), the definition of 'party' refers only to the appeals and references dealt with by the instrument and these definitions cease to be operative once one steps outside such appeals and references. In this regard see *A. B. Law* v. *Minister for Local Government and Traditional Homes Ltd.* (unreported: judgment delivered by Deale J. in the High Court on 9 May 1974) and in particular at pp. 4-5 of the judgment as follows: 'These meanings which are highly artificial are, of course, confined to the statutory instrument in which they are used. Once one steps outside the instrument, these meanings disappear and are replaced by the ordinary meaning of the word party as used in litigation, or quasi-litigation, such as the inspector's hearing, or by lawyers in their ordinary parlance. It is, of course, clear beyond yea or nay that within article 2 (ii) the plaintiff is not or was not a party. But that does not, in my opinion, mean that he cannot maintain this action. To test his right to sue, one must look far beyond article 2 (ii), and at the realities of the plaintiff's position in connection with the planning application, the appeal, and in this court'. See p. 34 ante.
33. Section 23 of the 1976 Act.
34. See judgment of Henchy J. in *Susan Geraghty* v. *Minister for Local Government* (1976 I R 153 at pp. 174-5). 'For these reasons I conclude that the appointed person *must* include in his report a fair and accurate summary of the evidence and submissions together with his findings of fact, and that he *may* include observations, inferences, submissions and recommendations limited to what took place at the hearing'.
35. Section 82 (3).
36. By S.I. no. 308 of 1976 the Board was established on 1 January 1977 and by S.I. no. 56 of 1977 it took seisin of appeals from 15 March 1977.
37. Section 29 of the 1963 Act.
38. This is one of the appeals which has not been removed from jurisdiction of the Minister by the 1976 Act.
39. See *Viscount Securities Ltd.* (unreported: judgment of Finaly P. delivered in the High Court 21 December 1976) for a detailed analysis and interpretation of section 55 (1) (a) of the 1963 Act which at first sight appears to exclude compensation in the vast majority of cases.
40. Section 71.
41. Section 72.
43. Section 73.

LIST OF CASES
(* denotes English and Scottish cases)

A. G. v. Simpson 1959 I R 105 11,12

Buckley & Others (Sinn Féin) v. Attorney General 1950 I R 67 6

Byrne v. Ireland 1972 I R 241 3,5,6,58

Camrose (Viscount) v. Basingstoke Corporation 1966 1 W L R 1100* 62

Cedars Rapids Manufacturing and Power Co. v. Lacarte 1914 A C 569* 27

Central Dublin Development Association Ltd. v. Attorney General 109 I L T R 69 4,57,64

Conway v. Rimmer 1968 A C 910* 12,13

Cooper v. Wandsworth Board of Works 1963 14 CB(NS) 180* 57,58

in re Deansrath Investment Co. Ltd. 1974 I R 228 26,27,28,60,62

Duncan v. Cammel Laird & Co. Ltd. 1942 A C 624* 11,12,60

D P P v. Ferguson (unreported: Irish Times 29 October 1975) 60

Dunne Ltd. v. Dublin Co. Co. 1974 I R 45. 66,67

East Donegal Co-Operative v. Attorney General 1970 I R 317 19,20,58,59

Educational Company of Ireland v. Fitzpatrick & Ors. 1961 I R 345 96 I L T R 147 58

Finn v. Bray U D C 1974 I R 169 63

Frescati Estates Ltd. v. Marie Walker 1975 I R 177 34,43,63,65,67

Fuller v. Dublin County Council 1976 I R 20 61

Geraghty v. Minister for Local Government 1976 I R 153 16,19,61,68

Gilford R D C v. Fortiscue* 1959 2 QB 112 65

Glasgow Corporation v. Central Land Board 1956 S C 1* 13

Glover v. B L N 1973 I R 388 59

in re Haughey 1971 I R 217 17

Hendron v. Dublin Corporation 62

Huntley v. Gaskell* 1905 2 Ch 656 29

International Trading Ltd. v. Corporation of Dublin 1974 I R 373 61

TABLE OF STATUTES
(English statutes marked thus *)

Index